Edging
Stitch Guide

LEISURE ARTS, INC.
Maumelle, Arkansas

EDITORIAL STAFF
Senior Product Director: Pam Stebbins
Editorial Production Director: Tona Jolly
Creative Art Director: Katherine Laughlin
Technical Writer: Linda A. Daley
Technical Editor: Sarah J. Green
Editorial Writer: Susan Frantz Wiles
Art Category Manager: Lora Puls
Graphic Artist: Lora Puls
Photography Technical Manager:
  Stephanie Johnson
Prepress Technician: Janie Marie Wright
Contributing Photographers:
  Jason Masters and Ken West
Contributing Photo Stylist: Lori Wenger

BUSINESS STAFF
President and Chief Executive Officer:
  Fred F. Pruss
Senior Vice President of Operations:
  Jim Dittrich
Vice President of Retail Sales:
  Martha Adams
Chief Financial Officer: Tiffany P. Childers
Controller: Teresa Eby
Information Technology Director:
  Brian Roden
Director of E-Commerce: Mark Hawkins
Manager of E-Commerce: Robert Young

Copyright © 2016 by Leisure Arts, Inc., 104 Champs Blvd., STE 100, Maumelle, AR 72113-6738, www.leisurearts.com. All rights reserved. This publication is protected under federal copyright laws. Reproduction or distribution of this publication or any other Leisure Arts publication, including publications which are out of print, is prohibited unless specifically authorized. This includes, but is not limited to, any form of reproduction or distribution on or through the Internet, including posting, scanning, or e-mail transmission.

We have made every effort to ensure that these instructions are accurate and complete. We cannot, however, be responsible for human error, typographical mistakes, or variations in individual work.

ISBN-13/EAN: 978-1-4647-3884-5
UPC: 0-28906-75541-1

Library of Congress Control Number: 2015955192

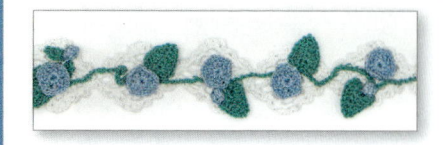

Meet the Designer: Terry Kimbrough

Known best for her romantic, vintage-inspired crochet designs, Terry Kimbrough loves making and using edgings.

"I can slip a zipper bag with a ball of thread and a hook into my purse and I'm ready to use those bits of time spent waiting," she said. "I wish I had logged the miles of edging I've done this way! I especially like to add an edging to a purchased item, such as tea towels, or a flannel blanket for a new baby. It's a quick and easy way to personalize gifts and make them extra-special."

A former technical writer for Leisure Arts, Terry learned to crochet at the age of 4 or 5 by imitating her grandmother.

"Thread was my first love," she said, "and then I went through an extended afghan phase, and then came the baby layette phase. Right now, I'm working on patterns to inspire children to learn to crochet."

To find more of Terry's designs, visit LeisureArts.com.

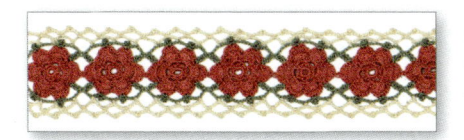

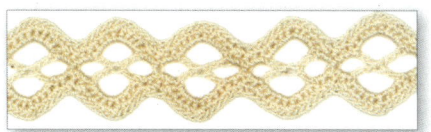

PAINTED DAISIES 4	PICOT MESH 47
FLORAL FILIGREE 6	GARDENIAS 48
ORNATE SCALLOPS 8	DAISIES 50
BRACELET 11	PANSIES 52
ROSY TRELLIS 12	FORGET-ME-NOTS 55
FILET DIAMONDS 14	DAFFODILS 56
GRAPES 16	SUNFLOWERS 58
ZIGZAG 19	VINTAGE FLOWERS 60
PINEAPPLES 20	PETUNIAS 62
PRETTY PICOTS 23	MORNING GLORIES 64
SPIDERWEBS 24	WISPY LACE 66
FLORAL STENCIL 26	POINSETTIAS 67
BORDER ROSES 28	BACHELOR BUTTONS 70
VIOLETS 30	FUCHSIAS 72
LOVELY LACE 32	IRISH ROSES 74
RUFFLED SCALLOPS 33	SPRING BEAUTY 76
WILD ROSES 34	CHRYSANTHEMUMS 77
PICKET FENCE 36	ANTIQUE BLOSSOMS 80
POSIES 37	COSMOS 83
VINTAGE RINGS 38	BROWN-EYED SUSANS 85
PEARL DROPS 39	VICTORIAN ROSEBUDS 87
HOLLY 40	POPCORN BAND 90
STAR FLOWERS 42	PICOT BAND 91
TINY FLOWERS 44	RICKRACK LACE 92
INSERTION LACE 45	GENERAL INSTRUCTIONS 93
LEAVES 46	THREAD INFORMATION 96

3

PAINTED DAISIES

Approximate Width: 1 5/8" (4.25 cm)

STITCH GUIDE

PICOT
Ch 3, sc in third ch from hook.

FIRST MOTIF

Rnd 1 (Right side)**:** With Yellow, ch 2, 6 sc in second ch from hook; join with slip st to first sc, finish off.

Note: Loop a short piece of thread around any stitch to mark Rnd 1 as **right** side.

Rnd 2: With **right** side facing, join Blue or Pink with sc in any sc *(see Joining With Sc, page 94)*; ch 9, sc in same st, ch 9, (sc, ch 9) twice in each sc around; join with slip st to first sc, finish off: 12 ch-9 sps.

Rnd 3: With **right** side facing, join White with sc in any ch-9 sp; work Picot, (sc in next ch-9 sp, work Picot) around; join with slip st to first sc, place marker in any Picot made for joining placement, finish off.

ADDITIONAL MOTIFS

Work same as First Motif through Rnd 2, alternating colors on Rnd 2: 12 ch-9 sps.

Rnd 3 (Joining rnd)**:** With **right** side facing, join White with sc in any ch-9 sp; (work Picot, sc in next ch-9 sp) 6 times, place marker in last Picot made for joining placement, (work Picot, sc in next ch-9 sp) 3 times, ch 1; holding Motifs with **wrong** sides together, sc in marked Picot on **previous Motif**, ch 1, sc in ch **before** joining sc on **new Motif**, ★ sc in next ch-9 sp, ch 1, sc in next Picot on **previous Motif**, ch 1, sc in ch **before** joining sc on **new Motif**; repeat from ★ once **more**; join with slip st to first sc, finish off.

Make as many Additional Motifs as needed for desired length less 1⅝" (4.25 cm), working an odd number of Additional Motifs.

LAST MOTIF

Work same as First Motif through Rnd 2, using opposite color used on Rnd 2 of previous Motif: 12 ch-9 sps.

Rnd 3 (Joining rnd)**:** With **right** side facing, join White with sc in any ch-9 sp; (work Picot, sc in next ch-9 sp) 9 times, ch 1; holding Motifs with **wrong** sides together, sc in marked Picot on **previous Motif**, ch 1, sc in ch **before** joining sc on **new Motif**, ★ sc in next ch-9 sp, ch 1, sc in next Picot on **previous Motif**, ch 1, sc in ch **before** joining sc on **new Motif**; repeat from ★ once **more**; join with slip st to first sc, finish off.

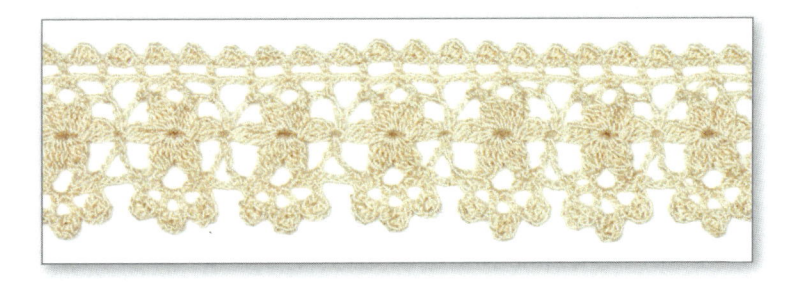

FLORAL FILIGREE

Approximate Width: 2¼" (5.75 cm)

STITCH GUIDE

3-TR CLUSTER (uses one st)
★ YO twice, insert hook in st indicated, YO and pull up a loop, (YO and draw through 2 loops on hook) twice; repeat from ★ 2 times **more**, YO and draw through all 4 loops on hook.

4-TR CLUSTER (uses one st)
★ YO twice, insert hook in st indicated, YO and pull up a loop, (YO and draw through 2 loops on hook) twice; repeat from ★ 3 times **more**, YO and draw through all 5 loops on hook.

INSTRUCTIONS

Foundation Row (Right side)**:**
★ Ch 5, work 3-tr Cluster in fifth ch from hook; repeat from ★ across for desired length, ending by working an even number of 3-tr Clusters; do **not** finish off.

Note: Loop a short piece of thread around any stitch to mark Foundation Row as **right** side.

Rnd 1: Ch 5, (work 4-tr Cluster, ch 5) twice in ch at base of first 3-tr Cluster, sc in ch at base of next 3-tr Cluster, ★ ch 5, (work 4-tr Cluster, ch 5) twice in ch at base of next 3-tr Cluster, sc in ch at base of next 3-tr Cluster; repeat from ★ across, ch 5, tie a scrap piece of thread around last ch-5 made to mark Upper Edging placement; working across opposite side of Foundation Row, (work 4-tr Cluster, ch 5) twice in ch at base of next 3-tr Cluster, † sc in ch at base of next 3-tr Cluster, ch 5, (work 4-tr Cluster, ch 5) twice in ch at base of next 3-tr Cluster †; repeat from † to † across; join with slip st to top of last Cluster on Foundation Row; do **not** finish off.

UPPER EDGING

Row 1: Turn; slip st in first ch-5 sp, ch 6, sc in next ch-5 sp, ch 3, ★ (dc in next ch-5 sp, ch 3) twice, sc in next ch-5 sp, ch 3; repeat from ★ across to marked ch-5 sp, dc in marked sp.

Row 2: Ch 7, turn; 2 dc in fourth ch from hook, dc in next sc, ch 4, 2 dc in fourth ch from hook, ★ (dc in next dc, ch 4, 2 dc in fourth ch from hook) twice, dc in next sc, ch 4, 2 dc in fourth ch from hook; repeat from ★ across, skip next 2 chs, dc in next ch; finish off.

LOWER EDGING

With **right** side facing, join thread with slip st in first ch-5 sp; ch 1, sc in same sp, dc in next ch-5 sp, (ch 4, 2 dc in fourth ch from hook, dc in same sp) 3 times, sc in next ch-5 sp, ★ ch 3, sc in next ch-5 sp, dc in next ch-5 sp, (ch 4, 2 dc in fourth ch from hook, dc in same sp) 3 times, sc in next ch-5 sp; repeat from ★ across; finish off.

ORNATE SCALLOPS

Approximate Width: 3½" (9 cm)

ADDITIONAL SUPPLIES: ¼" (6 mm) wide ribbon - desired length

STITCH GUIDE

TREBLE CROCHET (abbreviated tr)
YO twice, insert hook in st indicated, YO and pull up a loop (4 loops on hook), (YO and draw through 2 loops on hook) 3 times.

DOUBLE TREBLE CROCHET (abbreviated dtr)
YO 3 times, insert hook in sp indicated, YO and pull up a loop (5 loops on hook), (YO and draw through 2 loops on hook) 4 times.

2-DC CLUSTER (uses one sp)
★ YO, insert hook in sp indicated, YO and pull up a loop, YO and draw through 2 loops on hook; repeat from ★ once **more**, YO and draw through all 3 loops on hook.

3-DC CLUSTER (uses one sp)
★ YO, insert hook in sp indicated, YO and pull up a loop, YO and draw through 2 loops on hook; repeat from ★ 2 times **more**, YO and draw through all 4 loops on hook.

5-DTR CLUSTER (uses one sp)
★ YO 3 times, insert hook in sp indicated, YO and pull up a loop, (YO and draw through 2 loops on hook) 3 times; repeat from ★ 4 times **more**, YO and draw through all 6 loops on hook.

PICOT
Ch 4, sc in fourth ch from hook.

MOTIF

Ch 10; join with slip st to form a ring.

Row 1: Ch 1, sc in ring, (ch 5, sc in ring) 6 times, ch 2, dc in ring to form last ch-5 sp: 7 ch-5 sps.

Row 2 (Right side)**:** Ch 7, turn; work 5-dtr Cluster in next ch-5 sp, (ch 7, work 5-dtr Cluster in next ch-5 sp) 4 times, ch 2, dtr in last ch-5 sp: 5 Clusters and 6 sps.

Note: Loop a short piece of thread around any stitch to mark Row 2 as **right** side.

Row 3: Ch 5, turn; 7 sc in next ch-7 sp, (ch 5, 7 sc in next ch-7 sp) 3 times, ch 2, dc in last ch-7 sp to form last ch-5 sp: 28 sc and 5 ch-5 sps.

Row 4: Ch 5, turn; sc in last ch-5 sp made, ch 5, skip next sc, sc in next 5 sc, ch 5, (sc in next ch-5 sp, ch 5, skip next sc, sc in next 5 sc, ch 5) 3 times, sc in last ch-5 sp, ch 2, dc in same sp to form last ch-5 sp: 10 ch-5 sps.

Row 5: Ch 5, turn; sc in next ch-5 sp, ch 5, skip next sc, sc in next 3 sc, ch 5, ★ (sc in next ch-5 sp, ch 5) twice, skip next sc, sc in next 3 sc, ch 5; repeat from ★ 2 times **more**, sc in next ch-5 sp, ch 2, dc in last ch-5 sp to form last ch-5 sp: 13 ch-5 sps.

Row 6: Ch 5, turn; sc in next ch-5 sp, (ch 5, sc in next ch-5 sp) across; finish off: 12 ch-5 sps.

Make as many Motifs as needed for desired length, allowing approximately ½" (12 mm) between each Motif.

UPPER EDGING

Row 1: With **right** side of any Motif facing and working across straight edge of Motif (end of rows), join thread with slip st in first ch-5 sp; ch 5 (**counts as first dc plus ch 2, now and throughout**), ★ † (dc in next ch-5 sp, ch 2) 3 times, (dc, ch 2) twice around next dtr, dc in next ch-5 sp, ch 2, (dc, ch 2) twice in ring, dc in next ch-5 sp, ch 2, (dc, ch 2) twice in next ch-7 sp †, (dc in next ch-5 sp, ch 2) 4 times, with **right** side of next Motif facing, dc in first ch-5 sp on next Motif, ch 2; repeat from ★ across to last Motif, then repeat from † to † once, dc in next ch-5 sp, (ch 2, dc in next ch-5 sp) 3 times.

Row 2: Ch 6, turn; tr in next dc, ch 4, sc in next dc, ch 4, tr in next dc, ★ (ch 2, tr in next dc) twice, ch 4, sc in next dc, ch 4, tr in next dc; repeat from ★ across.

Row 3: Ch 1, turn; sc in first tr, ch 5, skip next sc, sc in next tr, ★ (2 sc in next ch-2 sp, sc in next tr) twice, ch 5, skip next sc, sc in next tr; repeat from ★ across to last ch-sp, 3 sc in last sp.

Row 4 (Eyelet row): Ch 5, turn; skip next 2 sc, dc in next sc, ch 2, skip next 2 chs, dc in next ch, ch 2, dc in next sc, ★ (ch 2, skip next 2 sc, dc in next sc) twice, ch 2, skip next 2 chs, dc in next ch, ch 2, dc in next sc; repeat from ★ across.

Row 5: Ch 3, turn; work 2-dc Cluster in first ch-2 sp, ★ ch 4, sc in next ch-2 sp, ch 4, work 3-dc Cluster in next ch-2 sp; repeat from ★ across.

Row 6: Ch 1, turn; sc in first ch-4 sp, work Picot, sc in next ch-4 sp, ★ ch 2, sc in next ch-4 sp, work Picot, sc in next ch-4 sp; repeat from ★ across, sc in top of 2-dc Cluster; finish off.

LOWER EDGING

With **right** side facing, join thread with slip st in end of first row of Upper Edging; working across last row on each Motif, work (slip st, ch 3, 2-dc Cluster, Picot) in each of next 12 ch-5 sps, ★ skip next dc, work (slip st, ch 3, 2-dc Cluster, Picot) in next ch-2 sp (between Motifs), work (slip st, ch 3, 2-dc Cluster, Picot) in each of next 12 ch-5 sps; repeat from ★ across, slip st in end of first row of Upper Edging; finish off.

Weave ribbon through Eyelet row.

BRACELET

Approximate Width: 1" (2.5 cm)

INSTRUCTIONS

Row 1 (Right side)**:** With Rose, ch 4, 4 dc in fourth ch from hook, ★ ch 5, 4 dc in fourth ch from hook; repeat from ★ for desired length; finish off.

Note: Loop a short piece of thread around any stitch to mark Row 1 as **right** side.

Row 2: With **right** side facing, join Green with slip st in last dc worked; ch 3, 4 dc in same st, ch 1, slip st in ch at base of last 4 dc on Row 1, ★ ch 3, 4 dc in same ch, ch 1, slip st in ch at base of next 4 dc on Row 1; repeat from ★ across; finish off.

Row 3: With **right** side facing, join Ecru with sc in same ch as last slip st *(see Joining With Sc, page 94)*; ch 3, (sc, ch 3, sc) in top of beginning ch, † ch 5, (sc, ch 3, sc) in top of ch-3 on next group †; repeat from † to † across, ch 3, sc in same dc as joining on Row 2, ch 3, (sc, ch 3, sc) in top of ch-3 on first group on Row 2, repeat from † to † across, ch 3; join with slip st to first sc, finish off.

ROSY TRELLIS

Approximate Width: 2½" (6.25 cm)

STITCH GUIDE

CLUSTER (uses one st)
★ YO twice, insert hook in st indicated, YO and pull up a loop, (YO and draw through 2 loops on hook) twice; repeat from ★ once **more**, YO and draw through all 3 loops on hook.

FIRST ROSE

With Rose, ch 6; join with slip st to form a ring.

Rnd 1 (Right side)**:** Ch 1, 12 sc in ring; join with slip st to first sc.

Note: Loop a short piece of thread around any stitch to mark Rnd 1 as **right** side.

Rnd 2: Ch 1, sc in same st, ch 3, skip next sc, ★ sc in next sc, ch 3, skip next sc; repeat from ★ around; join with slip st to first sc: 6 ch-3 sps.

Rnd 3: Slip st in first ch-3 sp, ch 1, (sc, hdc, 3 dc, hdc, sc) in same sp and in each ch-3 sp around; join with slip st to first sc: 6 Petals.

Rnd 4: Ch 1, sc in same st, ch 4, skip next 6 sts, ★ sc in next sc keeping ch-4 **behind** Petal, ch 4, skip next 6 sts; repeat from ★ around; join with slip st to first sc keeping ch-4 **behind** Petal.

Rnd 5: Slip st in first ch-4 sp, ch 1, (sc, hdc, 5 dc, hdc, sc) in same sp and in each ch-4 sp around; join with slip st to first sc, finish off.

SECOND ROSE

Rnds 1-4: Work same as First Rose.

Rnd 5: Slip st in first ch-4 sp, ch 1, (sc, hdc, 3 dc) in same sp; with **right** side facing, slip st in center dc of any Petal on Rnd 5 of First Rose, (2 dc, hdc, sc) in same sp to complete Petal, (sc, hdc, 5 dc, hdc, sc) in next ch-4 sp and in each ch-4 sp around; join with slip st to first sc, finish off.

THIRD ROSE

Rnds 1-4: Work same as First Rose.

Rnd 5: Slip st in first ch-4 sp, ch 1, (sc, hdc, 3 dc) in same sp; with **right** side facing, skip next 2 Petals **after** last joining and slip st in center dc of next Petal, (2 dc, hdc, sc) in same sp to complete Petal, (sc, hdc, 5 dc, hdc, sc) in next ch-4 sp and in each ch-4 sp around; join with slip st to first sc, finish off.

Make and join more Roses, in same manner as Third Rose, for desired length.

EDGING

Rnd 1: With **right** side facing, skip next 2 Petals **after** last joining and join Green with slip st in center dc on next Petal; ch 1, (sc, ch 3, sc in third ch from hook, sc) in same st, ch 5, [(sc, ch 3, sc in third ch from hook, sc) in center dc on next Petal, ch 5] twice, † work Cluster in first sc on next Petal, skip joined Petal on next Rose and work Cluster in first sc on next Petal, ch 5, (sc, ch 3, sc in third ch from hook, sc) in center dc on same Petal, ch 5, ★ (sc, ch 3, sc in third ch from hook, sc) in center dc on next Petal, ch 5, work Cluster in first sc on next Petal, skip joined Petal on next Rose and work Cluster in first sc on next Petal, ch 5, (sc, ch 3, sc in third ch from hook, sc) in center dc on same Petal, ch 5; repeat from ★ across to last Rose †, [(sc, ch 3, sc in third ch from hook, sc) in center dc on next Petal, ch 5] 4 times, repeat from † to † once, (sc, ch 3, sc in third ch from hook, sc) in center dc on next Petal, ch 5; join with slip st to first sc, finish off.

Rnd 2: With **right** side facing, join Ecru with slip st in first ch of first ch-5 sp; ch 1, sc in same ch, ch 7, skip next 3 chs, sc in next ch, ch 7, sc in first ch of next ch-5 sp, ch 7, skip next 3 chs, sc in next ch, (ch 7, sc in center ch of next ch-5 sp) across to first ch-5 sp on last Rose, (ch 7, sc in first ch of next ch-5 sp, ch 7, skip next 3 chs, sc in next ch) 4 times, (ch 7, sc in center ch of next ch-5 sp) across to first ch-5 sp on last Rose, (ch 7, sc in first ch of next ch-5 sp, ch 7, skip next 3 chs, sc in next ch) twice, ch 4, dc in first sc to form last ch-7 sp.

Rnd 3: Ch 1, sc in last ch-7 sp made, ch 5, sc in third ch from hook, ch 2, ★ sc in next ch-7 sp, ch 5, sc in third ch from hook, ch 2; repeat from ★ around; join with slip st to first sc, finish off.

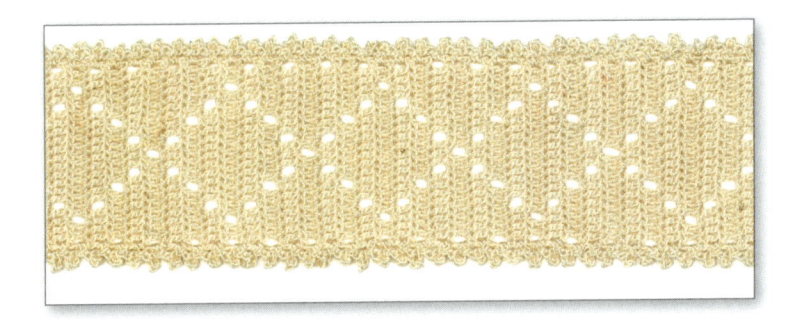

FILET DIAMONDS

Approximate Width: 3" (7.5 cm)

INSTRUCTIONS

Row 1 (Right side)**:** Ch 25, dc in fourth ch from hook and in each ch across: 23 sts.

Row 2: Ch 3 (**counts as first dc, now and throughout**), turn; dc in next 10 dc, ch 1, skip next dc, dc in last 11 sts: 22 dc.

Row 3: Ch 3, turn; dc in next 8 dc, ch 1, skip next dc, dc in next dc and in next ch-1 sp, dc in next dc, ch 1, skip next dc, dc in last 9 dc: 21 dc.

14 www.leisurearts.com

Row 4: Ch 3, turn; dc in next 6 dc, ch 1, skip next dc, dc in next dc and in next ch-1 sp, dc in next 3 dc and in next ch-1 sp, dc in next dc, ch 1, skip next dc, dc in last 7 dc.

Row 5: Ch 3, turn; dc in next 4 dc, ch 1, skip next dc, dc in next dc and in next ch-1 sp, dc in next 7 dc and in next ch-1 sp, dc in next dc, ch 1, skip next dc, dc in last 5 dc.

Row 6: Ch 3, turn; dc in next 2 dc, ch 1, skip next dc, dc in next dc and in next ch-1 sp, dc in next 11 dc and in next ch-1 sp, dc in next dc, ch 1, skip next dc, dc in last 3 dc.

Row 7: Ch 3, turn; dc in next 2 dc and in next ch-1 sp, dc in next dc, ch 1, skip next dc, dc in next 11 dc, ch 1, skip next dc, dc in next dc and in next ch-1 sp, dc in last 3 dc.

Row 8: Ch 3, turn; dc in next 4 dc and in next ch-1 sp, dc in next dc, ch 1, skip next dc, dc in next 7 dc, ch 1, skip next dc, dc in next dc and in next ch-1 sp, dc in last 5 dc.

Row 9: Ch 3, turn; dc in next 6 dc and in next ch-1 sp, dc in next dc, ch 1, skip next dc, dc in next 3 dc, ch 1, skip next dc, dc in next dc and in next ch-1 sp, dc in last 7 dc.

Row 10: Ch 3, turn; dc in next 8 dc and in next ch-1 sp, dc in next dc, ch 1, skip next dc, dc in next dc and in next ch-1 sp, dc in last 9 dc: 22 dc.

Repeat Rows 3-10 for desired length, ending by working Row 10.

Last Row: Ch 3, turn; dc in next 10 dc and in next ch-1 sp, dc in last 11 dc; do **not** finish off.

EDGING

Ch 1; working in end of rows, sc in first row, (ch 4, sc in fourth ch from hook, sc in next row) across; working in free loops of beginning ch *(Fig. 2, page 94)*, sc in first 23 chs; working in end of rows, sc in first row, (ch 4, sc in fourth ch from hook, sc in next row) across; working across sts on Last Row, sc in each dc across; join with slip st to first sc, finish off.

GRAPES

Approximate Width: 3" (7.5 cm)

STITCH GUIDE
TREBLE CROCHET
 (abbreviated tr)
YO twice, insert hook in st or sp indicated, YO and pull up a loop (4 loops on hook), (YO and draw through 2 loops on hook) 3 times.

CLUSTER *(uses one st)*
★ YO, insert hook in st indicated, YO and pull up a loop, YO and draw through 2 loops on hook; repeat from ★ 3 times **more**, YO and draw through all 5 loops on hook, ch 1 to close.

GRAPES

Row 1: With Lavender, ch 5, work 2 Clusters in fifth ch from hook: 2 Clusters.

Row 2 (Right side): Ch 1, turn; 2 sc in each Cluster across: 4 sc.

Note: Loop a short piece of thread around any stitch to mark Row 2 as **right** side.

Row 3: Ch 3, turn; work Cluster in each sc across: 4 Clusters.

Row 4: Ch 1, turn; 2 sc in first Cluster, sc in each Cluster across to last Cluster, 2 sc in last Cluster: 6 sc.

Rows 5-7: Repeat Rows 3 and 4 once, then repeat Row 3 once **more**: 8 Clusters.

Row 8: Ch 1, turn; sc in each Cluster across.

Row 9: Ch 3, turn; work Cluster in each sc across.

Row 10: Ch 1, turn; sc in first Cluster, skip next Cluster, sc in next 2 Clusters, ch 3, sc in next 2 Clusters, skip next Cluster, sc in last Cluster; finish off: 6 sc.

LEAF
Row 1: With Green, ch 11, sc in second ch from hook and in each ch across to last ch, 3 sc in last ch; working in free loops of beginning ch *(Fig. 2, page 94)*, sc in next 9 chs: 21 sc.

Row 2 (Right side)**:** Ch 4, turn; tr in first 3 sc, slip st around post of last tr made, dc in next 3 sc, slip st around post of last dc made, hdc in next 2 sc, slip st around post of last hdc made, sc in next sc, slip st in next 3 sc, sc in next sc, ch 1, hdc in next 2 sc, ch 1, dc in next sc, tie a scrap piece of thread around last dc made to mark joining, dc in next 2 sc, ch 1, tr in next 2 sc, (tr, ch 4, slip st) in last sc, slip st in end of beginning ch, ch 18 **very tightly**; finish off.

Note: Mark Row 2 as **right** side.

Make as many Grapes and Leaf sets as needed for desired length.

UPPER EDGING
Row 1: With **right** side of Leaf facing, join Ecru with slip st in marked dc; ch 6, skip next 2 dc, dc in next tr, ch 2; with **right** side of Grapes facing, holding Grapes in **front** of Leaf and working in ch-3 sp on Row 10 of Grapes **and** in second ch-4 sp on Leaf, (tr, ch 2) twice in next sp, skip next sc on Grapes, (tr, ch 2, tr) in next sc; ★ with **right** side of next Leaf facing, (tr, ch 2) twice in marked dc, skip next 2 dc on Leaf, dc in next tr, ch 2; with **right** side of next Grapes facing, holding Grapes in **front** of Leaf and working in ch-3 sp on Row 10 of Grapes **and** in second ch-4 sp on Leaf, (tr, ch 2) twice in next sp, skip next sc on Grapes, (tr, ch 2, tr) in next sc; repeat from ★ across remaining Grapes and Leaf sets, ch 2, skip next sc, tr in last sc on last set.

Row 2: Ch 5, turn; skip next 2 chs, (dc in next st, ch 2, skip next 2 chs) 6 times, dc in sp **between** next 2 tr *(Fig. 3, page 95)*, ★ ch 2, skip next 2 chs, (dc in next st, ch 2, skip next 2 chs) 5 times, dc in sp **between** next 2 tr; repeat from ★ across to last set, (ch 2, skip next 2 chs, dc in next st) 5 times.

Row 3: Ch 4, turn; 2 dc in first dc, (slip st, ch 4, 2 dc) in next dc and in each dc across, skip next 2 chs, slip st in next ch.

Row 4: Ch 5, turn; sc in next ch-4 sp, (ch 2, sc in next ch-4 sp) across.

Row 5: Ch 4, turn; 2 dc in first sc, (slip st, ch 4, 2 dc) in next sc and in each sc across, skip next 2 chs, slip st in next ch; do **not** finish off.

LOWER EDGING

Sc evenly across end of Upper Edging, ch 5, skip first Cluster row on first Grapes, (sc in next sc row, ch 5, skip next Cluster row) 4 times, sc in ch at tip of Grapes, (ch 5, skip next Cluster row, sc in next sc row) 4 times, ch 3, skip next 6 sts on first Leaf, sc in next hdc, ★ ch 3, skip first Cluster row on next Grapes, (sc in next sc row, ch 5, skip next Cluster row) 4 times, sc in ch at tip of Grapes, (ch 5, skip next Cluster row, sc in next sc row) 4 times, ch 3, skip next 6 sts on next Leaf, sc in next hdc; repeat from ★ across; finish off.

ZIGZAG

Approximate Width: 1 1/8" (2.75 cm)

STITCH GUIDE
TREBLE CROCHET
(abbreviated tr)
YO twice, insert hook in st or sp indicated, YO and pull up a loop (4 loops on hook), (YO and draw through 2 loops on hook) 3 times.

INSTRUCTIONS

Foundation Row: With Green, ch 5, sc in second ch from hook, hdc in next ch, dc in next ch, tr in next ch (**first point made**), ★ ch 4, **turn**; sc in second ch from hook, hdc in next ch, dc in next ch, tr in next tr (**next point made**); repeat from ★ for desired length, working an odd number of points: finish off.

EDGING

Rnd 1 (Right side)**:** Join Ecru with slip st in top of last tr made; ch 4, 4 tr over post of same st, (sc in tip of next point, 4 tr over post of tr on next point) across, ch 4, slip st in sp **between** tr and dc on first point *(Fig. 3, page 95)*, ch 4, sc in tip of first point, (4 tr over post of tr on next point, sc in tip of next point) across, ch 4; join with slip st in same st as joining.

Rnd 2: Ch 1, 4 sc in first ch-4 sp, sc in next 4 tr, (sc in next sc and in next 4 tr) across, 4 sc in each of next 2 ch-4 sps, sc in next sc, (sc in next 4 tr and in next sc) across, 4 sc in last ch-4 sp; join with slip st to first sc, finish off.

PINEAPPLES

Approximate Width: 3¼" (8.25 cm)

STITCH GUIDE

TREBLE CROCHET (abbreviated tr)
YO twice, insert hook in sp indicated, YO and pull up a loop (4 loops on hook), (YO and draw through 2 loops on hook) 3 times.

SHELL (uses one st or sp)
(2 Dc, ch 2, 2 dc) in st or sp indicated.

PICOT
Ch 4, sc in fourth ch from hook.

FOUNDATION

Row 1: Ch 12, dc in sixth ch from hook, skip next 2 chs, work Shell in next ch, skip next 2 chs, dc in last ch.

Rows 2-4: Ch 3, turn; work Shell in next ch-2 sp, skip next 2 dc, dc in next st.

Row 5: Ch 7, turn; dc in first dc, work Shell in next ch-2 sp, skip next 2 dc, dc in next st.

Rows 6-8: Repeat Rows 2-4.

Row 9: Ch 5, turn; dc in first dc, work Shell in next ch-2 sp, skip next 2 dc, dc in next st.

Repeat Rows 2-9 for desired length, ending by working Row 9; do **not** finish off.

LOWER EDGING

Row 1 (Right side)**:** Ch 3, turn; sc in next ch-2 sp, ch 3, skip next 2 dc, sc in next dc, ch 3; working in end of rows, work Shell in first row (ch-5 sp), ★ ch 3, skip next 3 rows, 9 tr in next row (ch-7 sp), ch 3, skip next 3 rows, work Shell in next row (ch-5 sp); repeat from ★ across, dc in ch at base of first dc on Row 1 of Foundation.

Row 2: Ch 3, turn; work Shell in first ch-2 sp, ★ ch 3, (sc in next tr, ch 3) 9 times, skip next ch-3 sp, work Shell in next ch-2 sp; repeat from ★ across to last 3 sts, skip next 2 dc, dc in last st.

Row 3: Ch 3, turn; work Shell in first ch-2 sp, ★ ch 3, skip next ch-3 sp, (sc in next ch-3 sp, ch 3) 8 times, skip next ch-3 sp, work Shell in next ch-2 sp; repeat from ★ across to last 3 sts, skip next 2 dc, dc in last st.

Row 4: Ch 3, turn; work Shell in first ch-2 sp, ★ ch 3, skip next ch-3 sp, (sc in next ch-3 sp, ch 3) 7 times, skip next ch-3 sp, work Shell in next ch-2 sp; repeat from ★ across to last 3 sts, skip next 2 dc, dc in last st.

Row 5: Ch 3, turn; work Shell in first ch-2 sp, ★ ch 3, skip next ch-3 sp, (sc in next ch-3 sp, ch 3) 6 times, skip next ch-3 sp, work Shell in next ch-2 sp; repeat from ★ across to last 3 sts, skip next 2 dc, dc in last st.

Row 6: Ch 3, turn; (work Shell, ch 2, 2 dc) in first ch-2 sp, ★ ch 3, skip next ch-3 sp, (sc in next ch-3 sp, ch 3) 5 times, skip next ch-3 sp, (work Shell, ch 2, 2 dc) in next ch-2 sp; repeat from ★ across to last 3 sts, skip next 2 dc, dc in last st.

Row 7: Ch 3, turn; 2 dc in first ch-2 sp, work Shell in next ch-2 sp, ch 3, skip next ch-3 sp, (sc in next ch-3 sp, ch 3) 4 times, skip next ch-3 sp, ★ work Shell in each of next 2 ch-2 sps, ch 3, skip next ch-3 sp, (sc in next ch-3 sp, ch 3) 4 times, skip next ch-3 sp; repeat from ★ across to last 2 ch-2 sps, work Shell in next ch-2 sp, 2 dc in last ch-2 sp, skip next 2 dc, dc in last st.

Row 8: Ch 3, turn; ★ skip next 2 dc, (dc, ch 1, dc) in sp **before** next Shell *(Fig. 3, page 95)*, work Shell in next ch-2 sp, ch 3, skip next ch-3 sp, (sc in next ch-3 sp, ch 3) 3 times, skip next ch-3 sp, work Shell in next ch-2 sp; repeat from ★ across to last 5 sts, skip next 2 dc, (dc, ch 1, dc) in sp **before** next dc, skip next 2 dc, dc in last st.

Row 9: Ch 3, turn; dc in first ch-1 sp, (work Picot, dc in same sp) twice, work Shell in next ch-2 sp, ch 3, skip next ch-3 sp, (sc in next ch-3 sp, ch 3) twice, skip next ch-3 sp, work Shell in next ch-2 sp, dc in next ch-1 sp, ★ (work Picot, dc in same sp) 3 times, work Shell in next ch-2 sp, ch 3, skip next ch-3 sp, (sc in next ch-3 sp, ch 3) twice, skip next ch-3 sp, work Shell in next ch-2 sp, dc in next ch-1 sp; repeat from ★ across to last 2 sts, (work Picot, dc in same sp) twice, skip next dc, dc in last st; do **not** finish off.

UPPER EDGING

Ch 1; working in end of rows on Lower Edging and across beginning ch of Foundation, sc evenly across, (sc, ch 5, sc) in end of each row across Foundation; working in each ch-3 sp and in end of rows on Lower Edging, sc evenly across; finish off.

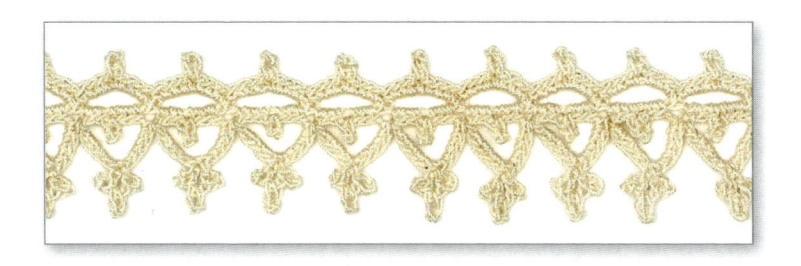

PRETTY PICOTS

Approximate Width: 1 3/8" (3.5 cm)

STITCH GUIDE
DOUBLE TREBLE CROCHET
(abbreviated dtr)
YO 3 times, insert hook in st indicated, YO and pull up a loop (5 loops on hook), (YO and draw through 2 loops on hook) 4 times.
PICOT
Ch 4, sc in fourth ch from hook.

INSTRUCTIONS

Foundation Row: Ch 7, dtr in seventh ch from hook, ★ ch 6, dtr in top of last dtr made; repeat from ★ for desired length; do **not** finish off.

Row 1: Ch 1, ★ (3 sc, work Picot, 3 sc) over post of next dtr, ch 9, **turn**; skip Picot and next 2 sc, slip st in next sc, **turn**; (5 sc, work 3 Picots, slip st in base of first Picot, 5 sc) in ch-9 sp; repeat from ★ across.

Row 2: Ch 1; working across opposite side of Foundation Row, (4 sc, work Picot, 4 sc) in each ch-6 sp across, slip st in first sc on Row 1; finish off.

SPIDERWEBS

Approximate Width: 4¼" (10.75 cm)

STITCH GUIDE

TREBLE CROCHET
(abbreviated tr)
YO twice, insert hook in sp indicated, YO and pull up a loop (4 loops on hook), (YO and draw through 2 loops on hook) 3 times.

DOUBLE TREBLE CROCHET
(abbreviated dtr)
YO 3 times, insert hook in st indicated, YO and pull up a loop (5 loops on hook), (YO and draw through 2 loops on hook) 4 times.

INSTRUCTIONS

Row 1 (Right side)**:** Ch 33, dc in sixth ch from hook and in next 3 chs, ch 2, skip next 2 chs, dc in next ch, ch 5, skip next 5 chs, dc in next ch, ch 3, skip next 2 chs, sc in next ch, ch 3, skip next 2 chs, dc in next ch, ch 5, skip next 5 chs, dc in next ch, ch 2, skip next 2 chs, dc in last ch.

Row 2: Ch 5 **(counts as first dc plus ch 2, now and throughout)**, turn; dc in next dc, ch 3, skip next 2 chs, sc in next ch, ch 3, dc in next dc, ch 5, skip next 2 ch-3 sps, dc in next dc, ch 2, skip next 2 chs, dc in next ch, ch 2, dc in next dc, 2 dc in next ch-2 sp, dc in next dc, ch 2, skip next 2 dc, dc in next dc, (3 dc, ch 2, tr) in last sp.

Row 3: Ch 5, turn; 3 dc in first ch-2 sp, dc in next dc, ch 5, tr in next ch-2 sp, ch 5, skip next 3 dc, dc in next dc, 2 dc in next ch-2 sp, dc in next dc, ch 2, dc in next dc, ch 3, skip next 2 chs, sc in next ch, ch 3, dc in next dc, ch 5, skip next 2 ch-3 sps, dc in next dc, ch 2, dc in last dc.

Row 4: Ch 5, turn; dc in next dc, ch 3, skip next 2 chs, sc in next ch, ch 3, dc in next dc, ch 5, skip next 2 ch-3 sps, dc in next dc, 2 dc in next ch-2 sp, dc in next dc, ch 6, sc in next ch-5 sp and in next tr, sc in next ch-5 sp, ch 6, skip next 3 dc, dc in next dc, (3 dc, ch 2, tr) in last sp.

Row 5: Ch 5, turn; 3 dc in first ch-2 sp, dc in next dc, ch 7, sc in next ch-6 sp and in next 3 sc, sc in next ch-6 sp, ch 7, skip next 3 dc, dc in next dc, 3 dc in next ch-5 sp, ch 2, dc in next dc, ch 5, skip next 2 ch-3 sps, dc in next dc, ch 2, dc in last dc.

Row 6: Ch 5, turn; dc in next dc, ch 3, skip next 2 chs, sc in next ch, ch 3, dc in next dc, ch 5, skip next 3 dc, dc in next dc, 3 dc in next ch-7 sp, ch 6, skip next sc, sc in next 3 sc, ch 6, 3 dc in next ch-7 sp, dc in next dc, skip next 2 dc, dtr in next dc, leave remaining sp unworked.

Row 7: Ch 5, turn; skip next 3 dc, dc in next dc, 3 dc in next ch-6 sp, ch 6, skip next sc, sc in next sc, ch 6, 3 dc in next ch-6 sp, dc in next dc, ch 2, skip next 2 dc, dc in next dc, ch 3, skip next 2 chs, sc in next ch, ch 3, dc in next dc, ch 5, skip next 2 ch-3 sps, dc in next dc, ch 2, dc in last dc.

Row 8: Ch 5, turn; dc in next dc, ch 3, skip next 2 chs, sc in next ch, ch 3, dc in next dc, ch 5, skip next 2 ch-3 sps, (dc in next dc, ch 2) twice, skip next 2 dc, dc in next dc, 3 dc in next ch-6 sp, ch 2, 3 dc in next ch-6 sp, dc in next dc, skip next 2 dc, dtr in next dc, leave remaining sp unworked.

Row 9: Ch 5, turn; skip next 3 dc, dc in next dc, 2 dc in next ch-2 sp, dc in next dc, ch 2, skip next 2 dc, dc in next dc, ch 5, skip next dc, dc in next dc, ch 3, skip next 2 chs, sc in next ch, ch 3, dc in next dc, ch 5, skip next 2 ch-3 sps, dc in next dc, ch 2, dc in last dc.

Repeat Rows 2-9 for desired length, ending by working Row 9; do **not** finish off.

EDGING

Working in end of rows, (slip st, ch 3, 2 dc) in each row across to last row, slip st in last row, ch 1; working over beginning ch, 2 sc in first sp, 5 sc in next sp, 2 sc in each of next 2 sps, 5 sc in next sp, 2 sc in next sp, sc in free loops of next 4 chs *(Fig. 2, page 94)*; working in end of rows, ★ (slip st, ch 3, 2 dc) in each of next 4 rows, (slip st, ch 3, 2 dc) twice in next row, (slip st, ch 3, 2 dc) in each of next 3 rows; repeat from ★ across to last row, (slip st, 2 sc) in last row, sc in next 4 dc, 2 sc in next ch-2 sp, 5 sc in next ch-5 sp, 2 sc in each of next 2 ch-2 sps, 5 sc in next ch-5 sp, 2 sc in last ch-2 sp; join with slip st to first slip st, finish off.

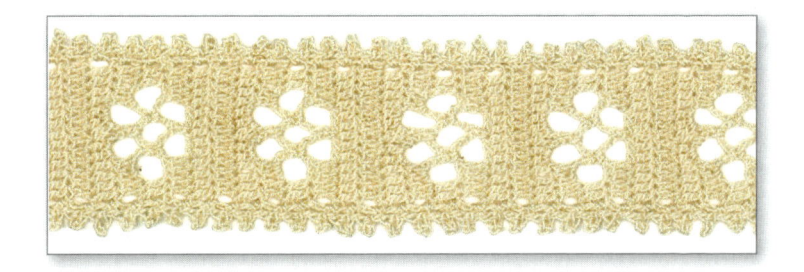

FLORAL STENCIL

Approximate Width: 2¼" (5.75 cm)

STITCH GUIDE

DECREASE (uses 2 sps)
YO, insert hook in **same** sp, YO and pull up a loop, YO and draw through 2 loops on hook, YO, insert hook in **next** sp, YO and pull up a loop, YO and draw through 2 loops on hook, YO and draw through all 3 loops on hook.

INSTRUCTIONS

Row 1 (Right side)**:** Ch 17, dc in fourth ch from hook and in each ch across: 15 sts.

Row 2: Ch 3 (**counts as first dc, now and throughout**), turn; dc in next 4 dc, ch 5, skip next 2 dc, sc in next dc, ch 5, skip next 2 dc, dc in next 4 dc and in next ch: 10 dc.

Row 3: Ch 3, turn; dc in next 2 dc, ch 5, (sc in next ch-5 sp, ch 5) twice, skip next 2 dc, dc in last 3 dc: 6 dc.

Row 4: Ch 3, turn; dc in next 2 dc, 2 dc in next ch-5 sp, ch 5, sc in next ch-5 sp, ch 5, 2 dc in next ch-5 sp, dc in last 3 dc: 10 dc.

Row 5: Ch 3, turn; dc in next 4 dc, 2 dc in next ch-5 sp, decrease, 2 dc in same ch-5 sp, dc in last 5 dc: 15 sts.

Rows 6 and 7: Ch 3, turn; dc in next st and in each st across.

Repeat Rows 2-7 for desired length, ending by working Row 5; do **not** finish off.

EDGING

Ch 1; † working in end of rows, sc in first row, (ch 4, sc in fourth ch from hook, sc in next row) across †; working in free loops of beginning ch *(Fig. 2, page 94)*, sc in first 15 chs, repeat from † to † once, sc in each dc across; join with slip st to first sc, finish off.

BORDER ROSES

Approximate Width: 2¼" (5.75 cm)

ADDITIONAL SUPPLIES: Tapestry needle

STITCH GUIDE
DOUBLE TREBLE CROCHET
(abbreviated dtr)
YO 3 times, insert hook in sp indicated, YO and pull up a loop (5 loops on hook), (YO and draw through 2 loops on hook) 4 times.

FLOWER
With Red and leaving a long end for sewing, ch 6; join with slip st to form a ring.

Rnd 1: Ch 1, (sc in ring, ch 4) 4 times; join with slip st to first sc: 4 ch-4 sps.

Rnd 2 (Right side)**:** Ch 1, (sc, 5 dc, sc) in each ch-4 sp around; join with slip st to first sc: 4 petals.

Note: Loop a short piece of thread around any stitch to mark Rnd 2 as **right** side.

Rnd 3: Ch 1; working **behind** petals and into beginning ring **below** each ch-4 on Rnd 1, sc in first sp, ch 4, (sc, ch 4) twice in next sp, sc in next sp, ch 4, (sc, ch 4) twice in next sp; join with slip st to first sc: 6 ch-4 sps.

Rnd 4: Ch 1, (sc, 7 dc, sc) in each ch-4 sp around; join with slip st to first sc, finish off: 6 petals.

Using photo as a guide, twist first petal on Rnd 2 over beginning ring and sew in place.

Make as many Flowers as needed for desired length, working an even number of Flowers and allowing approximately ¾" (19 mm) between each Flower.

JOINING

With **right** side of first Flower facing, join Green with slip st in center dc of any petal; ch 1, (sc, ch 5, sc) in same st, (ch 7, sc, ch 5, sc) in center dc on each of next 2 petals, ch 7; with **wrong** side of **next** Flower facing, (sc, ch 5, sc) in center dc of any petal, † (ch 7, sc, ch 5, sc) in center dc on each of next 2 petals, ch 7; with **right** side of **next** Flower facing, (sc, ch 5, sc) in center dc on any petal, (ch 7, sc, ch 5, sc) in center dc on each of next 2 petals, ch 7; with **wrong** side of **next** Flower facing, (sc, ch 5, sc) in center dc of any petal †; repeat from † to † across to last Flower, (ch 7, sc, ch 5, sc) in center dc on each of next 5 petals, ch 4, sc around ch-7 between Flowers, ch 3; with **right** side of **next** Flower facing, (sc, ch 5, sc) in center dc on next petal, (ch 7, sc, ch 5, sc) in center dc on each of next 2 petals, ★ ch 4, sc around ch-7 between Flowers, ch 3; with **wrong** side of **next** Flower facing, (sc, ch 5, sc) in center dc on next petal, (ch 7, sc, ch 5, sc) in center dc on each of next 2 petals, ch 4, sc around ch-7 between Flowers, ch 3; with **right** side of **next** Flower facing, (sc, ch 5, sc) in center dc on next petal, (ch 7, sc, ch 5, sc) in center dc on each of next 2 petals; repeat from ★ across, ch 7; join with slip st to first sc, finish off.

EDGING

Row 1: With **right** side facing, join Ecru with slip st in first ch-5 sp after joining; ch 13, sc in next ch-5 sp, ch 8, dtr in next ch-5 sp, ★ ch 2, dtr in next ch-5 sp, ch 8, sc in next ch-5 sp, ch 8, dtr in next ch-5 sp; repeat from ★ across long edge.

Row 2: Ch 5, turn; skip next 2 chs, (dc in next ch, ch 2, skip next 2 chs) twice, dc in next sc, ch 2, skip next 2 chs, (dc in next ch, ch 2, skip next 2 chs) twice, ★ (dc in next dtr, ch 2) twice, skip next 2 chs, (dc in next ch, ch 2, skip next 2 chs) twice, dc in next sc; repeat from ★ across to last ch-sp, (ch 2, skip next 2 chs, dc in next ch) 3 times.

Row 3: Ch 1, turn; (sc, ch 5, sc) in each ch-sp across; finish off.

VIOLETS

Approximate Width: 2" (5 cm)

STITCH GUIDE
TREBLE CROCHET
(abbreviated tr)
YO twice, insert hook in sp indicated, YO and pull up a loop (4 loops on hook), (YO and draw through 2 loops on hook) 3 times.

FLOWER
With Lavender, ch 6; join with slip st to form a ring.

Rnd 1: Ch 1, (sc in ring, ch 5) 5 times; join with slip st to first sc: 5 ch-5 sps.

Rnd 2 (Right side)**:** (Slip st, ch 2, 12 dc, ch 2, slip st) in each of first 3 ch-5 sps, (slip st, ch 3, 7 tr, ch 1, 7 tr, ch 3, slip st) in each of last 2 ch-5 sps **(large petals made)**; join with slip st to first slip st, finish off.

Note: Loop a short piece of thread around any stitch to mark Rnd 2 as **right** side.

Make as many Flowers as needed for desired length, allowing approximately ½" (12 mm) between each Flower.

EDGING

Rnd 1: With **right** side facing, skip first tr on first large petal and join Ecru with sc in next tr *(see Joining With Sc, page 94)*; ch 5, skip next 2 tr, sc in next tr, ch 5, sc in next ch-1 sp, ch 5, skip next 2 tr, sc in next tr, ch 5, skip first 4 tr on next large petal and sc in next tr, ch 5, sc in next ch-1 sp, ★ (ch 5, skip next 2 tr, sc in next tr) twice, ch 3, skip first tr on first large petal on **next** Flower, (sc in next tr, ch 5, skip next 2 tr) twice, sc in next ch-1 sp, ch 5, skip next 2 tr, sc in next tr, ch 5, skip first 4 tr on next large petal and sc in next tr, ch 5, sc in next ch-1 sp; repeat from ★ across each Flower, ch 5, skip next 2 tr, sc in next tr, ch 2, skip next 2 tr, dc in next tr to form last ch-5 sp.

Rnd 2: Ch 1, turn; sc in last ch-5 sp made, (ch 3, sc in next ch-5 sp) twice, dc in next ch-5 sp, (ch 1, dc in same sp) 6 times, ★ (sc in next ch-5 sp, ch 3) twice, skip next 3 ch-sps, sc in next ch-5 sp, ch 3, sc in next ch-5 sp, dc in next ch-5 sp, (ch 1, dc in same sp) 6 times; repeat from ★ across to last 3 ch-5 sps, sc in next ch-5 sp, ch 3, sc in next ch-5 sp, ch 1, hdc in last ch-5 sp to form last ch-3 sp.

Rnd 3: Ch 8, turn; sc in fifth ch from hook, tr in next ch-3 sp, ch 2, sc in next ch-1 sp, (ch 3, sc in next ch-1 sp) 5 times, ch 2, tr in next ch-3 sp, ch 4, sc in top of tr just made, ★ skip next ch-3 sp, tr in next ch-3 sp, ch 2, sc in next ch-1 sp, (ch 3, sc in next ch-1 sp) 5 times, ch 2, tr in next ch-3 sp, ch 4, sc in top of tr just made; repeat from ★ across to last ch-3 sp, tr in last ch-3 sp; finish off.

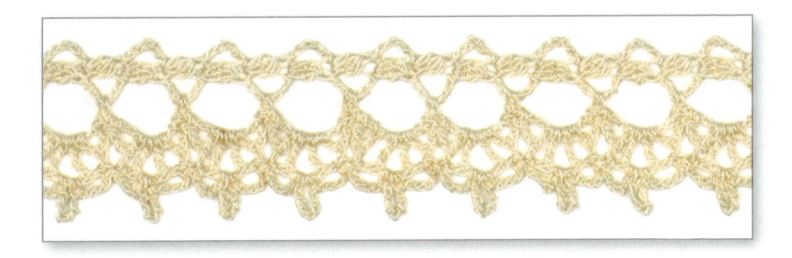

LOVELY LACE

Approximate Width: 1 5/8" (4.25 cm)

STITCH GUIDE

TREBLE CROCHET (abbreviated tr)
YO twice, insert hook in sp indicated, YO and pull up a loop (4 loops on hook), (YO and draw through 2 loops on hook) 3 times.

3-DC CLUSTER (uses one st)
★ YO, insert hook in st indicated, YO and pull up a loop, YO and draw through 2 loops on hook; repeat from ★ 2 times **more**, YO and draw through all 4 loops on hook.

FOUNDATION

Row 1: Ch 8, work 3-dc Cluster in eighth ch from hook.

Row 2: Ch 7, turn; work 3-dc Cluster in top of 3-dc Cluster.

Repeat Row 2 for desired length, ending by working an odd number of rows; do **not** finish off.

EDGING

Row 1 (Right side)**:** Ch 3, turn; working in end of rows, sc in first row (ch-7 sp), ★ ch 9, skip next row, sc in next row (ch-7 sp); repeat from ★ across long edge.

Row 2: Ch 1, turn; in each ch-9 sp across work **[**sc, ch 2, dc, ch 2, (tr, ch 2) twice, dc, ch 2, sc**]**, slip st in last sc.

Row 3: Ch 3, turn; skip first ch-2 sp, sc in next ch-2 sp, ch 5, (sc, ch 7, sc) in next ch-2 sp, ch 5, sc in next ch-2 sp, ★ skip next 2 ch-2 sps, sc in next ch-2 sp, ch 5, (sc, ch 7, sc) in next ch-2 sp, ch 5, sc in next ch-2 sp; repeat from ★ across to last ch-2 sp, ch 3, skip last ch-2 sp, slip st in last sc; finish off.

RUFFLED SCALLOPS

Approximate Width: 1" (2.5 cm)

STITCH GUIDE
TREBLE CROCHET
 (abbreviated tr)
YO twice, insert hook in st or sp indicated, YO and pull up a loop (4 loops on hook), (YO and draw through 2 loops on hook) 3 times.

INSTRUCTIONS

Scallop Row (Right side)**:** Ch 6, [tr, (ch 1, tr) 6 times] in sixth ch from hook (**Scallop made**), ★ ch 5, **turn**; dc in first tr, ch 5, **turn**; [tr, (ch 1, tr) 6 times] in ch-5 sp (**Scallop made**); repeat from ★ for desired length; finish off.

Note: Loop a short piece of thread around any stitch to mark Scallop Row as **right** side.

EDGING

With **right** side facing, join thread with slip st around beginning ch-6; ch 1, (sc, ch 3) twice around same ch, (sc in next ch-1 sp, ch 3) 6 times, ★ sc around post of next dc, ch 3, (sc, ch 3) twice in next ch-5 sp, (sc in next ch-1 sp, ch 3) 6 times; repeat from ★ across; working across opposite side, (sc, ch 3) 3 times around post of tr, sc in same sp as tr, ch 3, [sc in last ch-3 sp on same Scallop **and** over first tr on next Scallop, ch 3, sc in same sp as tr, ch 3] across; join with slip st to first sc.

Last Row: Ch 1, turn; (sc, ch 4, sc in fourth ch from hook, sc) in first ch-3 sp and in each ch-3 sp across long edge; finish off.

WILD ROSES

Approximate Width: 1 3/8" (3.5 cm)

STITCH GUIDE

CLUSTER (uses one sp)
★ YO twice, insert hook in sp indicated, YO and pull up a loop, (YO and draw through 2 loops on hook) twice; repeat from ★ once **more**, YO and draw through all 3 loops on hook.
PICOT
Ch 2, slip st in top of Cluster just made.

FIRST MOTIF

Rnd 1 (Right side)**:** With Yellow, ch 2, 6 sc in second ch from hook; join with slip st to first sc.

Note: Loop a short piece of thread around any stitch to mark Rnd 1 as **right** side.

Rnd 2: Ch 1, sc in same st, ch 3, (sc in next sc, ch 3) around; join with slip st to first sc, finish off: 6 ch-3 sps.

Rnd 3: With **right** side facing, join Pink with sc in any ch-3 sp *(see Joining With Sc, page 94)*; (5 dc, sc) in same sp (**petal made**), (sc, 5 dc, sc) in each ch-3 sp around; join with slip st to first sc, finish off: 6 petals.

Rnd 4: With **right** side facing, join Green with sc in sp **before** first sc on any petal *(Fig. 3, page 95)*; ch 3, keeping petals to **front** of work, skip petal, ★ sc in sp **before** first sc on next petal, ch 3, skip petal; repeat from ★ around; join with slip st to first sc: 6 ch-3 sps.

Rnd 5: Slip st in first ch-3 sp, † work (ch 4, Cluster, Picot, ch 4, slip st) twice in same sp †, place marker in last Picot made for joining placement, ch 3, (sc in next ch-3 sp, ch 3) 3 times, slip st in next ch-3 sp, repeat from † to † once, ch 3, sc in last ch-3 sp, ch 3; join with slip st to first slip st, finish off.

ADDITIONAL MOTIFS

Work same as First Motif through Rnd 4: 6 ch-3 sps.

Rnd 5 (Joining rnd)**:** Slip st in first ch-3 sp, work (ch 4, Cluster, Picot, ch 4, slip st) twice in same sp, place marker in last Picot made for joining placement, ch 3, (sc in next ch-3 sp, ch 3) 3 times, slip st in next ch-3 sp, ch 4, work Cluster in same sp, ch 1; holding Motifs with **wrong** sides together, slip st in marked Picot on **previous Motif**, ch 1, slip st in top of last Cluster made on **new Motif**, ch 4, work (slip st, ch 4, Cluster, Picot, ch 4, slip st) in same sp, ch 3, sc in last ch-3 sp, ch 3; join with slip st to first slip st, finish off.

Make as many Additional Motifs as needed for desired length less 2" (5 cm).

LAST MOTIF

Work same as First Motif through Rnd 4: 6 ch-3 sps.

Rnd 5 (Joining rnd)**:** Slip st in first ch-3 sp, work (ch 4, Cluster, Picot, ch 4, slip st) twice in same sp, ch 3, (sc in next ch-3 sp, ch 3) 3 times, slip st in next ch-3 sp, ch 4, work Cluster in same sp, ch 1; holding Motifs with **wrong** sides together, slip st in marked Picot on **previous Motif**, ch 1, slip st in last Cluster made on **new Motif**, ch 4, work (slip st, ch 4, Cluster, Picot, ch 4, slip st) in same sp, ch 3, sc in last ch-3 sp, ch 3; join with slip st to first slip st, finish off.

PICKET FENCE

Approximate Width: 2¼" (5.75 cm)

INSTRUCTIONS

Row 1 (Right side)**:** Ch 14, dc in fourth ch from hook and in each ch across: 12 sts.

Note: Loop a short piece of thread around any stitch to mark Row 1 as **right** side.

Row 2: Ch 13, turn; skip first 11 dc, dc in next ch.

Row 3: Ch 3, turn; dc in next 11 chs: 12 sts.

Repeat Rows 2 and 3 for desired length, ending by working Row 3 and a minimum of 5 rows; finish off.

UPPER EDGING

Row 1: With **wrong** side facing and working in end of rows, join thread with slip st in first row; ch 4, (dc, ch 1, dc) in same row, sc in next row, ★ dc in next row, (ch 1, dc in same row) 4 times, sc in next row; repeat from ★ across to last row, dc in last row, (ch 1, dc in same row) twice.

Row 2: Ch 5, turn; sc in first ch-1 sp, ch 3, sc in next 2 ch-1 sps, ch 3, sc in next ch-1 sp, ch 5, ★ sc in next ch-1 sp, ch 3, sc in next 2 ch-1 sps, ch 3, sc in next ch-1 sp, ch 5; repeat from ★ across, sc in next ch; finish off.

LOWER EDGING

Repeat Upper Edging across opposite side.

POSIES

FLOWER

With Rose, ch 6; join with slip st to form a ring.

Rnd 1: Ch 1, (sc, ch 3) 6 times in ring; join with slip st to first sc: 6 ch-3 sps.

Rnd 2 (Right side)**:** Ch 1, (sc, 5 dc, sc) in each ch-3 sp around; join with slip st to first sc, finish off: 6 petals.

Note: Loop a short piece of thread around any stitch to mark Rnd 2 as **right** side.

Make as many Flowers as needed for desired length, allowing approximately ¾" (19 mm) between each Flower.

Approximate Width: 1¾" (4.5 cm)

EDGING

Row 1: With **wrong** side of Flower facing, join Green with sc in center dc of any petal *(see Joining With Sc, page 94)*; ch 7, (sc, ch 5, sc) in center dc of next petal, ch 7, sc in center dc of next petal, ★ ch 5, with **wrong** side of **next** Flower facing, sc in center dc of any petal, ch 7, (sc, ch 5, sc) in center dc of next petal, ch 7, sc in center dc of next petal; repeat from ★ for remaining Flowers.

Row 2: Ch 3, turn; 8 dc in first ch-7 sp, (3 dc, ch 2, 3 dc) in next ch-5 sp, 8 dc in next ch-7 sp, dc in next sc, ★ sc in next ch-5 sp, dc in next sc, 8 dc in next ch-7 sp, (3 dc, ch 2, 3 dc) in next ch-5 sp, 8 dc in next ch-7 sp, dc in next sc; repeat from ★ across; finish off.

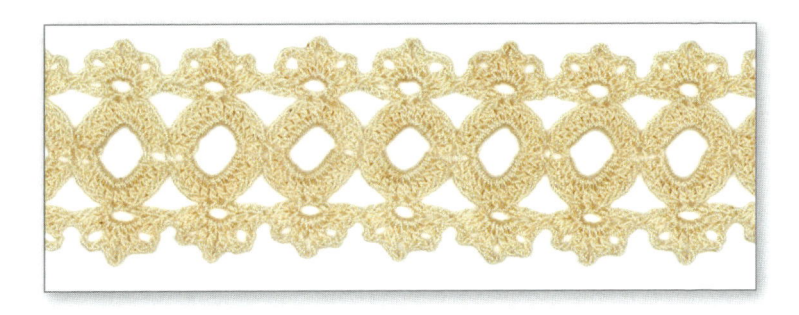

VINTAGE RINGS

Approximate Width: 2" (5 cm)

STITCH GUIDE
DOUBLE TREBLE CROCHET
(abbreviated dtr)
YO 3 times, insert hook in st indicated, YO and pull up a loop (5 loops on hook), (YO and draw through 2 loops on hook) 4 times.

BASE
Foundation Row: Ch 6, dtr in sixth ch from hook, (ch 11, dtr in sixth ch from hook) across for desired length plus approximately 2" (5 cm).

Rnd 1 (Right side)**:** Ch 3 **(counts as first dc, now and throughout)**, working over posts of dtr, 11 dc around first dtr, (skip next 2 chs, slip st in next ch, 12 dc around next dtr) across; working over beginning ch on opposite side of Foundation Row, 12 dc in first sp, ★ skip next 2 chs, slip st in free loop of next ch *(Fig. 2, page 94)*, 12 dc in next sp; repeat from ★ across; join with slip st to first dc, do **not** finish off.

EDGING
Rnd 1: Slip st in next 5 dc, ch 1, sc in same st, ch 4, sc in next dc, ch 7, (skip first 5 dc of next circle, sc in next dc, ch 4, sc in next dc, ch 7) across long edge to last circle, (skip next 4 dc, sc in next dc, ch 4, sc in next dc, ch 7) twice, (skip first 5 dc of next circle, sc in next dc, ch 4, sc in next dc, ch 7) across long edge to last circle, skip next 4 dc, sc in next dc, ch 4, sc in next dc, ch 7; join with slip st to first sc.

Rnd 2: (Slip st, ch 3, dc) in first ch-4 sp, (ch 3, 2 dc in same sp) 3 times, skip next 3 chs, slip st in next ch, ★ 2 dc in next ch-4 sp, (ch 3, 2 dc in same sp) 3 times, skip next 3 chs, slip st in next ch; repeat from ★ around; join with slip st to first dc, finish off.

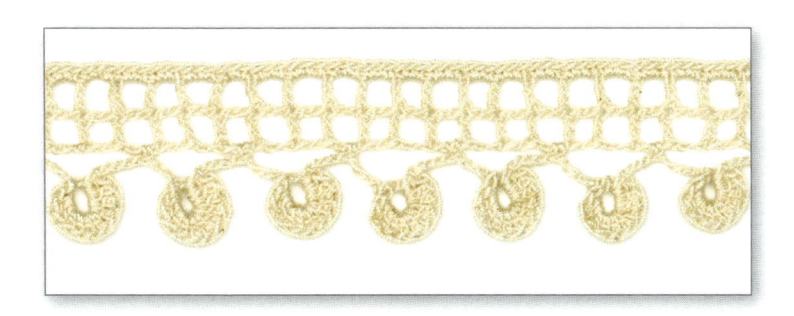

PEARL DROPS

Approximate Width: 1½" (3.75 cm)

FOUNDATION

Row 1: Ch 11, dc in eighth ch from hook, ch 2, skip next 2 chs, dc in last ch: 2 ch-sps.

Row 2: Ch 5, turn; dc in next dc, ch 2, skip next 2 chs, dc in next ch.

Repeat Row 2 for desired length, ending by working a multiple of 3 + 1 row; do **not** finish off.

EDGING

Ch 1; working in end of rows, sc in first row, ★ ch 10, slip st in sixth ch from hook to form a ring, (sc, hdc, 9 dc, hdc, sc) in ring, ch 4, skip next 2 rows, sc in next row; repeat from ★ across, sc evenly across beginning ch of Foundation, 3 sc in end of each row across, sc evenly across last row of Foundation; join with slip st to first sc, finish off.

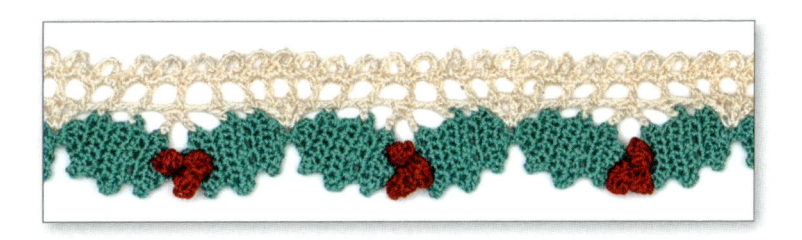

HOLLY

Approximate Width: 1¾" (4.5 cm)

ADDITIONAL SUPPLIES: Tapestry needle

STITCH GUIDE

DECREASE
Pull up a loop in each of next 2 sc, YO and draw through all 3 loops on hook.

DOUBLE DECREASE
Pull up a loop in each of next 3 sts, YO and draw through all 4 loops on hook.

CLUSTER (uses next 2 points)
★ YO twice, insert hook in **next** point, YO and pull up a loop, (YO and draw through 2 loops on hook) twice; repeat from ★ once **more**, YO and draw through all 3 loops on hook.

LEAVES

Row 1: With Green, ch 2, 3 sc in second ch from hook.

Row 2: Ch 1, turn; sc in each sc across.

Row 3 (Right side)**:** Ch 1, turn; 2 sc in first sc, sc in next sc, 2 sc in last sc: 5 sc.

Note: Loop a short piece of thread around any stitch to mark Row 3 as **right** side.

Row 4: Ch 1, turn; 3 sc in first sc, sc in next 3 sc, 3 sc in last sc: 9 sc.

Row 5: Turn; slip st in first 3 sc, ch 1, sc in same st and in next 4 sc, leave remaining 2 sc unworked: 5 sc.

Row 6: Ch 1, turn; 2 sc in first sc, sc in next 3 sc, 2 sc in last sc: 7 sc.

Row 7: Ch 1, turn; 3 sc in first sc, sc in next 5 sc, 3 sc in last sc: 11 sc.

Row 8: Turn; slip st in first 2 sc, ch 1, decrease, double decrease, leave remaining 2 sc unworked: 3 sts.

Row 9: Ch 1, turn; 2 sc in first st, sc in next st, 2 sc in last st: 5 sc.

Row 10: Ch 1, turn; 3 sc in first sc, sc in next 3 sc, 3 sc in last sc: 9 sc.

Row 11: Turn; slip st in first 2 sc, ch 1, decrease, sc in next sc, decrease, leave remaining 2 sc unworked: 3 sts.

Row 12: Ch 1, turn; double decrease: one st.

Row 13: Ch 1, turn; 3 sc in st: 3 sc.

Repeat Rows 2-13 for desired length, ending by working Row 12 and an even number of Leaves; finish off.

EDGING

Row 1: With **right** side facing, join Ecru with sc in last st made *(see Joining With Sc, page 94)*; ch 2, sc in next point, ch 2, dc in next point, ch 2, work Cluster, ch 2, dc in next point, ch 2, sc in next point, ★ (ch 2, dc) 3 times in st between Leaves, ch 2, sc in next point, ch 2, dc in next point, ch 2, work Cluster, ch 2, dc in next point, ch 2, sc in next point; repeat from ★ across, ch 2, sc in end of last Leaf.

Row 2: Ch 6, turn; skip next 2 chs, dc in next st, ★ ch 3, skip next 2 chs, dc in next st; repeat from ★ across.

Row 3: Ch 1, turn; (sc, ch 5, sc) in each ch-3 sp across, slip st in third ch of turning ch; finish off.

BERRIES

With Red, ★ ch 4, 4 dc in fourth ch from hook, drop loop from hook, insert hook in top of beginning ch-4, hook dropped loop and draw through st; repeat from ★ 2 times **more**, ch 1; finish off leaving a long end for sewing.

Make additional Berries as needed.

Using photo as a guide for placement, sew Berries to each pair of Leaves.

STAR FLOWERS

Approximate Width: 2 1/8" (5.5 cm)

STITCH GUIDE

BEGINNING POPCORN
Ch 3 **(counts as first dc, now and throughout)**, 4 dc in ring, drop loop from hook, insert hook in first dc of 5-dc group, hook dropped loop and draw through st.

POPCORN
5 Dc in ring, drop loop from hook, insert hook in first dc of 5-dc group, hook dropped loop and draw through st.

PICOT
Ch 4, sc in fourth ch from hook.

Note: Loop a short piece of thread around any stitch to mark Rnd 1 as **right** side.

FIRST MOTIF

With White, ch 5; join with slip st to form a ring.

Rnd 1 (Right side)**:** Work beginning Popcorn, ch 3, (work Popcorn, ch 3) 4 times; join with slip st to top of beginning Popcorn, finish off: 5 ch-3 sps.

Rnd 2: With **right** side facing, join Green with sc in any ch-3 sp *(see Joining With Sc, page 94)*; ch 3, ★ (sc, ch 3) twice in next ch-3 sp, (sc, ch 3) 3 times in next ch-3 sp; repeat from ★ once **more**, sc in same sp as first sc, dc in first sc to form last ch-3 sp: 12 ch-3 sps.

Rnd 3: Ch 3, (dc, ch 3, 2 dc) in last ch-3 sp made **(corner made)**, (ch 3, sc in next ch-3 sp) twice, (ch 3, 2 dc) twice in next ch-3 sp, place marker in last ch-3 made for joining placement, ch 3, (sc in next ch-3 sp, ch 3) twice, ★ (2 dc, ch 3) twice in next ch-3 sp, (sc in next ch-3 sp, ch 3) twice; repeat from ★ once **more**; join with slip st to first dc, finish off: 16 ch-3 sps.

ADDITIONAL MOTIFS

Work same as First Motif through Rnd 2: 12 ch-3 sps.

Rnd 3 (Joining rnd)**:** Ch 3, (dc, ch 3, 2 dc) in last ch-3 sp made, (ch 3, sc in next ch-3 sp) twice, (ch 3, 2 dc) twice in next ch-3 sp, place marker in last ch-3 made for joining placement, ch 3, (sc in next ch-3 sp, ch 3) twice, (2 dc, ch 3) twice in next ch-3 sp, (sc in next ch-3 sp, ch 3) twice, 2 dc in next ch-3 sp, ch 1; holding Motifs with **wrong** sides together, sc in marked ch-3 sp on **previous Motif**, ch 1, 2 dc in same sp on **new Motif**, ch 3, (sc in next ch-3 sp, ch 3) twice; join with slip st to first dc, finish off.

Make as many Additional Motifs as needed for desired length less 2" (5 cm).

LAST MOTIF

Work same as First Motif through Rnd 2: 12 ch-3 sps.

Rnd 3 (Joining rnd)**:** Ch 3, (dc, ch 3, 2 dc) in last ch-3 sp made, ch 3, (sc in next ch-3 sp, ch 3) twice, ★ (2 dc, ch 3) twice in next ch-3 sp, (sc in next ch-3 sp, ch 3) twice; repeat from ★ once **more**, 2 dc in next ch-3 sp, ch 1; holding Motifs with **wrong** sides together, sc in marked ch-3 sp on **previous Motif**, ch 1, 2 dc in same sp on **new Motif**, (ch 3, sc in next ch-3 sp) twice, ch 1, hdc in first dc to form last ch-3 sp; do **not** finish off.

BORDER

Ch 1, sc in last ch-3 sp made, work Picot, (sc, work Picot) twice in next ch-3 sp, † [(sc in next ch-3 sp, work Picot) 3 times, (sc, work Picot) twice in next ch-3 sp] 2 times, sc in next ch-3 sp, (work Picot, sc in next ch-3 sp) twice, skip next joining, ★ (sc in next ch-3 sp, work Picot) 3 times, (sc, work Picot, sc) in next ch-3 sp, (work Picot, sc in next ch-3 sp) 3 times, skip next joining; repeat from ★ across to last Motif †, (sc in next ch-3 sp, work Picot) 3 times, (sc, work Picot) twice in next ch-3 sp, repeat from † to † once, (sc in next ch-3 sp, work Picot) twice; join with slip st to first sc, finish off.

TINY FLOWERS

Approximate Width: 1 1/8" (2.75 cm)

FOUNDATION
FIRST FLOWER
With Pink, ch 4; join with slip st to form a ring.

Rnd 1 (Right side): Ch 1, sc in ring, ch 3, place marker around ch-3 just made for Border placement, sc in ring, (ch 3, sc in ring) 4 times, ch 1, hdc in first sc to form last ch-3 sp; do **not** finish off.

Note: Loop a short piece of thread around any stitch to mark Rnd 1 as **right** side.

ADDITIONAL FLOWERS
Rnd 1: Ch 5, slip st in fourth ch from hook to form a ring, ch 1, skip joining, (sc in ring, ch 3) twice, place marker around last ch-3 made for Border placement, (sc in ring, ch 3) 3 times, place marker around last ch-3 made for Border placement, sc in ring, ch 1, hdc in first sc to form last ch-3 sp; do **not** finish off.

Make as many Additional Flowers as needed for desired length less 1" (2.5 cm).

LAST FLOWER
Rnd 1: Ch 5, slip st in fourth ch from hook to form a ring, ch 1, skip joining, (sc in ring, ch 3) 3 times, place marker around last ch-3 made for Border placement, (sc in ring, ch 3) 3 times; join with slip st to first sc, finish off.

BORDER
Rnd 1: With **right** side facing, join White with sc in marked ch-3 sp on First Flower *(see Joining With Sc, page 94)*; ch 4, (skip next ch-3 sp, sc in next ch-3 sp, ch 4) twice, (sc in marked ch-3 sp on next Flower, ch 4) across to Last Flower, sc in marked ch-3 sp on Last Flower, (ch 4, skip next ch-3 sp, sc in next ch-3 sp) twice, (ch 4, sc in marked ch-3 sp on next Flower) across, ch 1, dc in first sc to form last ch-4 sp.

Rnd 2: Ch 1, [sc, (ch 3, sc) twice] in last ch-4 sp made and in each ch-4 sp around; join with slip st to first sc, finish off.

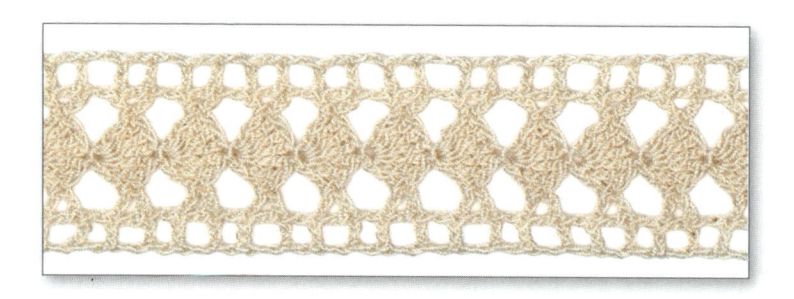

INSERTION LACE

Approximate Width: 1 3/8" (3.5 cm)

STITCH GUIDE
TREBLE CROCHET
(abbreviated tr)
YO twice, insert hook in st indicated, YO and pull up a loop (4 loops on hook), (YO and draw through 2 loops on hook) 3 times.

INSTRUCTIONS

Row 1: Ch 21, dc in eighth ch from hook, ch 5, skip next 4 chs, sc in next ch, ch 5, skip next 4 chs, dc in next ch, ch 2, skip next 2 chs, dc in last ch: 4 ch-sps.

Row 2 (Right side): Ch 5 **(counts as first dc plus ch 2, now and throughout)**, turn; dc in next dc, ch 2, sc in next ch-5 sp, 5 tr in next sc, sc in next ch-5 sp, ch 2, dc in next dc, ch 2, skip next 2 chs, dc in next ch.

Row 3: Ch 5, turn; dc in next dc, ch 5, skip next 2 tr, sc in next tr, ch 5, dc in next dc, ch 2, dc in last dc.

Row 4: Ch 5, turn; dc in next dc, ch 2, sc in next ch-5 sp, 5 tr in next sc, sc in next ch-5 sp, (ch 2, dc in next dc) twice.

Repeat Rows 3 and 4 for desired length, ending by working Row 3; finish off.

LEAVES

Approximate Width: 1¼" (3.25 cm)

STITCH GUIDE
TREBLE CROCHET
(abbreviated tr)
YO twice, insert hook in st indicated, YO and pull up a loop (4 loops on hook), (YO and draw through 2 loops on hook) 3 times.

FIRST LEAF

Ch 10, sc in second ch from hook, hdc in next ch, dc in next ch, tr in next 5 chs, (tr, dc, ch 3, slip st) in last ch, ch 4; working in free loops of beginning ch *(Fig. 2, page 94)*, skip first 4 chs, tr in next ch, leave remaining chs unworked; do **not** finish off.

SECOND LEAF

Ch 13, sc in second ch from hook, hdc in next ch, dc in next ch, tr in next 5 chs, (tr, dc, ch 3, slip st) in next ch, ch 4, leave last 3 chs unworked; working in free loops of worked ch, skip next 4 chs, tr in next ch.

Repeat Second Leaf until edging is desired length; do **not** finish off.

EDGING

Row 1: Ch 1, turn; sc in first ch-4 sp, ch 3, ★ working **over** 3 unworked chs between Leaves **and** in ch-3 sp on Leaf, sc in next ch-3 sp, ch 3, sc in next ch-4 sp, ch 3; repeat from ★ across to last Leaf, sc in ch-3 sp of last Leaf.

Row 2 (Right side)**:** Turn; (slip st, ch 3, 2 dc) in first ch-3 sp and in each ch-3 sp across, slip st in last sc.

Row 3: Turn; slip st in first 2 dc and in top of next ch-3, ch 1, (sc, ch 3, sc in third ch from hook, sc) in same st, ★ ch 2, (sc, ch 3, sc in third ch from hook, sc) in top of next ch-3; repeat from ★ across; finish off.

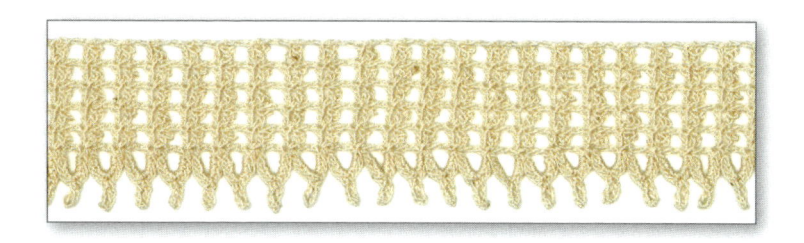

PICOT MESH

Approximate Width: 2" (5 cm)

STITCH GUIDE
PICOT
Ch 3, sc in third ch from hook.

INSTRUCTIONS
Row 1 (Right side)**:** Ch 17, sc in second ch from hook, ★ work Picot, skip next 2 chs, sc in next ch; repeat from ★ across: 5 Picots.

Row 2: Ch 5 **(counts as first dc plus ch 2)**, turn; skip first Picot, (dc in next sc, ch 2, skip next Picot) 4 times, (dc, ch 6, slip st) in last sc, **turn**; (4 sc, ch 7, sc in seventh ch from hook, 4 sc) in ch-6 sp, slip st in next dc.

Row 3: Ch 1, sc in same dc, ★ work Picot, skip next ch-2 sp, sc in next dc; repeat from ★ across: 5 Picots.

Repeat Rows 2 and 3 for desired length, ending by working Row 2; finish off.

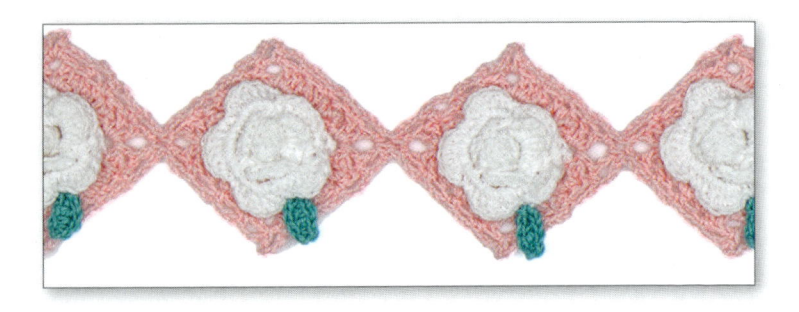

GARDENIAS

Approximate Width: 2¹/₈" (5.5 cm)

SQUARE
CENTER
Row 1 (Right side)**:** With White, ch 4, 6 dc in fourth ch from hook, drop loop from hook, insert hook in first dc of 6-dc group, hook dropped loop and draw through st, ch 3, slip st in ch at base of 6-dc group.

Note: Loop a short piece of thread around any stitch to mark Row 1 as **right** side.

Begin working in rounds.

Rnd 1: Ch 1, sc in same ch, ch 3, (sc in next ch-3 sp, ch 3) twice; join with slip st to first sc: 3 ch-3 sps.

Rnd 2: Slip st in first ch-3 sp, ch 1, (sc, 5 dc, sc) in same sp and in next 2 ch-3 sps; join with slip st to first sc: 15 dc and 6 sc.

Rnd 3: Ch 1, sc in sp **before** first sc *(Fig. 3, page 95)*, ch 3, skip next 7 sts, ★ sc in sp **before** next sc, ch 3, skip next 3 sts, sc in ch-3 sp on Rnd 1 **before** next dc, ch 3, skip next 3 sts; repeat from ★ once **more**; join with slip st to first sc: 5 ch-3 sps.

Rnd 4: Slip st in first ch-3 sp, ch 1, (sc, 5 dc, sc) in same sp and in each ch-3 sp around; join with slip st to first sc: 25 dc and 10 sc.

Rnd 5: Ch 1, sc in sp **before** first sc, ch 3, skip next 7 sts, ★ sc in sp **before** next sc, ch 3, skip next 7 sts; repeat from ★ around, place marker around last sc made for Leaf placement; join with slip st to first sc, finish off: 5 ch-3 sps.

48 www.leisurearts.com

Rnd 6: With **right** side facing, join Pink with sc in first ch-3 sp *(see Joining With Sc, page 94)*; (ch 3, sc in same sp) 3 times, ★ ch 3, sc in next ch-3 sp, (ch 3, sc in same sp) twice; repeat from ★ around, dc in first sc to form last ch-3 sp: 16 ch-3 sps.

Rnd 7: Ch 3 **(counts as first dc)**, (dc, ch 2, 2 dc) in last ch-3 sp made, place marker in ch-2 sp just made for Border placement, hdc in next ch-3 sp, sc in next ch-3 sp, hdc in next ch-3 sp, ★ (2 dc, ch 2, 2 dc) in next ch-3 sp, hdc in next ch-3 sp, sc in next ch-3 sp, hdc in next ch-3 sp; repeat from ★ 2 times **more**; join with slip st to first dc, finish off.

LEAF

With **right** side facing, join Green with slip st in marked sc on Rnd 5; working in back ridge of chs *(Fig. 1, page 94)*, ch 5, sc in second ch from hook, dc in last 3 chs; join with slip st to same st as joining, finish off.

Make as many Squares as needed for desired length, allowing approximately 1/8" (3 mm) between each Square.

BORDER

Joining Rnd: With **right** side of each Square facing, join Pink with sc in marked ch-2 sp on First Square; ch 5, sc in same sp, ★ ch 3, skip next st, (sc in next st, ch 3, skip next st) 3 times, (sc, ch 5, sc) in next ch-2 sp, ch 3, skip next st, (sc in next st, ch 3, skip next st) 3 times, sc in next ch-2 sp on same Square **and** in marked ch-2 sp on next Square; repeat from ★ across, ch 3, skip next st, (sc in next st, ch 3, skip next st) 3 times, [(sc, ch 5, sc) in next ch-2 sp, ch 3, skip next st, (sc in next st, ch 3, skip next st) 3 times] 3 times, † sc in same sp as joining on same Square **and** in same sp as joining on next Square, ch 3, skip next st, (sc in next st, ch 3, skip next st) 3 times, (sc, ch 5, sc) in next ch-2 sp, ch 3, skip next st, (sc in next st, ch 3, skip next st) 3 times †; repeat from † to † across; join with slip st to first sc, finish off.

DAISIES

Approximate Width: 2" (5 cm)

FIRST FLOWER

Rnd 1 (Right side)**:** With Yellow, ch 2, 8 hdc in second ch from hook; join with slip st to first hdc, finish off.

Note: Loop a short piece of thread around any stitch to mark Rnd 1 as **right** side.

Rnd 2: With **right** side facing, join White with slip st in any hdc; ★ † ch 7, working in back ridge of chs *(Fig. 1, page 94)*, sc in second ch from hook, hdc in next ch, dc in last 4 chs †, slip st in next hdc **(petal made)**; repeat from ★ 6 times **more**, place marker in unworked ch at tip of last petal made for joining placement, then repeat from † to † once; join with slip st to first slip st, finish off.

ADDITIONAL FLOWERS

Work same as First Flower through Rnd 1: 8 hdc.

Rnd 2 (Joining rnd)**:** With **right** side facing, join White with slip st in any hdc; † ch 7, working in back ridge of chs, sc in second ch from hook, hdc in next ch, dc in last 4 chs, slip st in next hdc †; repeat from † to † 3 times **more**, place marker in unworked ch at tip of last petal made for st placement, repeat from † to † once, ch 6; holding Flowers with **wrong** sides together, sc in unworked ch at tip of marked petal on **previous Flower**, working in back ridge of chs, sc in next ch on **new Flower**, hdc in next ch, dc in last 4 chs, slip st in next hdc, repeat from † to † once, ch 6, skip next petal on **previous Flower**, sc in

50 www.leisurearts.com

unworked ch at tip of next petal, working in back ridge of chs, sc in next ch on **new Flower**, hdc in next ch, dc in last 4 chs; join with slip st to first slip st, finish off.

Make as many Additional Flowers as needed for desired length less 1½" (3.75 cm).

LAST FLOWER
Work same as First Flower through Rnd 1: 8 hdc.

Rnd 2 (Joining rnd)**:** With **right** side facing, join White with slip st in any hdc; † ch 7, working in back ridge of chs, sc in second ch from hook, hdc in next ch, dc in last 4 chs, slip st in next hdc †; repeat from † to † 4 times **more**, ch 6; holding Flowers with **wrong** sides together, sc in unworked ch at tip of marked petal on **previous Flower**, working in back ridge of chs, sc in next ch on **new Flower**, hdc in next ch, dc in last 4 chs, slip st in next hdc, repeat from † to † once, ch 6, skip next petal on **previous Flower**, sc in unworked ch at tip of next petal, working in back ridge of chs, sc in next ch on **new Flower**, hdc in next ch, dc in last 4 chs; join with slip st to first slip st, finish off.

BORDER
Row 1: With **right** side of Flowers facing, join Blue with slip st in second petal **before** joining on First Flower; ch 8 (**counts as first dc plus ch 5**), sc in unworked ch at tip of next petal, ch 5, ★ dc in next joining sc, ch 5, sc in unworked ch at tip of next petal, ch 5; repeat from ★ across to last 4 petals on Last Flower, dc in unworked ch at tip of next petal, leave remaining petals unworked.

Row 2: Ch 1, turn; sc in first dc, ★ ch 2, skip next 2 chs, sc in next ch, ch 2, skip next 2 chs, sc in next st; repeat from ★ across.

Row 3: Turn; slip st in first ch-2 sp, ch 1, (sc, ch 3, sc) in same sp and in each ch-2 sp across; finish off.

PANSIES

Approximate Width: 1⅞" (4.75 cm)

STITCH GUIDE

TREBLE CROCHET
(abbreviated tr)
YO twice, insert hook in sp indicated, YO and pull up a loop (4 loops on hook), (YO and draw through 2 loops on hook) 3 times.

V-ST (uses one ch-3 sp)
(Dc, ch 2, dc) in ch-3 sp indicated.

FIRST PANSY

With Black, ch 5; join with slip st to form a ring.

Rnd 1 (Right side)**:** Ch 1, (sc in ring, ch 3) 3 times, (sc in ring, ch 5) twice; join with slip st to first sc, finish off: 5 sps.

Note: Loop a short piece of thread around any stitch to mark Rnd 1 as **right** side.

Rnd 2: With **right** side facing, join Purple with slip st in last ch-5 sp made; ch 3, tr in same sp, (ch 1, tr in same sp) 6 times, ch 3, slip st in same sp **(large petal made)**, sc in next sc, 3 dc in next ch-3 sp, place marker around last dc made for Leaf placement, 2 dc in same sp **(small petal made)**, sc in next sc, (5 dc in next ch-3 sp, sc in next sc) twice, slip st in next ch-5 sp, ch 3, tr in same sp, (ch 1, tr in same sp) 3 times, place marker around last ch-1 made for Border placement, (ch 1, tr in same sp) 3 times, ch 3, slip st in same sp changing to Yellow *(Fig. 4,* *page 95)*, working **around** center, insert hook in second ch-3 sp, YO and pull up a loop changing to Purple, YO and draw through both loops on hook; join with slip st to first slip st, finish off.

ADDITIONAL PANSIES
FLOWER
Work same as First Pansy through Rnd 1: 5 sps.

Rnd 2: With **right** side facing, join Purple with slip st in last ch-5 sp made; ch 3, tr in same sp, (ch 1, tr in same sp) 6 times, ch 3, slip st in same sp **(large petal made)**, sc in next sc, 3 dc in next ch-3 sp, place marker around last dc made for Leaf placement, 2 dc in same sp **(small petal made)**, (sc in next sc, 5 dc in next ch-3 sp) twice, **turn**; skip first 5 dc, working in sp **before** next sc, dc in sc one rnd **below** sc, place marker around post of dc just made for Leaf joining placement, **turn**; sc in next sc, slip st in next ch-5 sp, ch 3, tr in same sp, (ch 1, tr in same sp) 3 times, place marker around last ch-1 made for Border placement, (ch 1, tr in same sp) 3 times, ch 3, slip st in same sp changing to Yellow, working **around** center, insert hook in second ch-3 sp, YO and pull up a loop changing to Purple, YO and draw through both loops on hook; join with slip st to first slip st, finish off.

LEAF
With Green, ch 7; with **wrong** side of Flower facing, slip st around post of marked dc for Leaf joining placement, ch 3, **turn**; dc in first 4 chs of beginning ch-7, hdc in next 2 chs, 3 sc in last ch; working in free loops of beginning ch *(Fig. 2, page 94)*, hdc in next ch, with **right** side of **previous Flower** facing, slip st in marked dc for Leaf placement, sc in same ch on Leaf, hdc in next ch, dc in last 4 chs, ch 3, slip st in same ch; join with slip st around post of same dc as first slip st on **new Flower**, finish off.

Make as many Additional Pansies as needed for desired length less 1½" (3.75 cm).

LAST PANSY

Work same as First Pansy through Rnd 1: 5 sps.

Rnd 2: With **right** side facing, join Purple with slip st in last ch-5 sp made; ch 3, tr in same sp, (ch 1, tr in same sp) 6 times, ch 3, slip st in same sp **(large petal made)**, [sc in next sc, 5 dc in next ch-3 sp **(small petal made)**] 3 times, **turn**; skip first 5 dc, working in sp **before** next sc, dc in sc one rnd **below** sc, place marker around post of dc just made for Leaf joining placement, **turn**; sc in next sc, slip st in next ch-5 sp, ch 3, tr in same sp, (ch 1, tr in same sp) 3 times, place marker around last ch-1 made for Border placement, (ch 1, tr in same sp) 3 times, ch 3, slip st in same sp changing to Yellow, working **around** center, insert hook in second ch-3 sp and pull up a loop changing to Purple, YO and draw through both loops on hook; join with slip st to first slip st, finish off.

Work one Leaf.

BORDER

Row 1: With **right** side facing, join Ecru with sc in marked ch-1 sp on First Pansy *(see Joining With Sc, page 94)*; ch 3, sc in next ch-1 sp, ch 3, skip first ch-1 sp on **next** petal, ★ (sc in next ch-1 sp, ch 3) 3 times, sc in marked ch-1 sp on next Flower, ch 3, sc in next ch-1 sp, ch 3, skip first ch-1 sp on **next** petal; repeat from ★ across, sc in next ch-1 sp, (ch 3, sc in next ch-1 sp) twice, leave remaining ch-1 sps unworked.

Row 2: Turn; slip st in first ch-3 sp, ch 5 **(counts as first dc plus ch 2)**, dc in same sp, work V-St in next ch-3 sp and in each ch-3 sp across.

Row 3: Turn; slip st in first ch-2 sp, ch 1, (sc, ch 3, sc) in same sp and in each ch-2 sp across; finish off.

FORGET-ME-NOTS

Approximate Width: 1¼" (3.25 cm)

ADDITIONAL SUPPLIES: Tapestry needle

FLOWERS

With Blue, ch 4, ★ † (2 dc, ch 3, slip st) in fourth ch from hook, (ch 3, 2 dc, ch 3, slip st) 3 times in same ch **(4 petals made)**, ch 3 †, 3 dc in same ch, ch 8; repeat from ★ as many times as needed to reach desired length less ⅞" (22 mm), then repeat from † to † once, (2 dc, ch 3, slip st) in same ch; finish off.

Note: Loop a short piece of thread around any stitch to mark **right** side.

CENTER

Thread tapestry needle with Yellow and stitch **tightly** through center of first Flower (at base of sts) completely covering center; finish off.

Repeat in each Flower across.

BORDER

Row 1: With **right** side facing, join White with sc in second dc of first petal made on last Flower worked *(see Joining With Sc, page 94)*; (ch 5, sc in next dc on next petal) twice, ch 1, sc in second dc of first petal made on next Flower, ★ (ch 5, sc in next dc on next petal) twice, ch 1, sc in second dc of first petal on next Flower; repeat from ★ across to last 4 petals on last Flower, ch 5, sc in next dc on next petal, ch 2, dc in next dc on next petal to form last ch-5 sp, leave remaining petals unworked.

Row 2: Ch 1, turn; sc in last ch-5 sp made, (ch 3, sc in next ch-5 sp) across.

Row 3: Ch 1, turn; 4 sc in first ch-3 sp and in each ch-3 sp across; finish off.

DAFFODILS

Approximate Width 2¼" (5.75 cm)

STITCH GUIDE

TREBLE CROCHET
  (abbreviated tr)
YO twice, insert hook in tips of both petals indicated, YO and pull up a loop (4 loops on hook), (YO and draw through 2 loops on hook) 3 times.

DOUBLE TREBLE CROCHET
  (abbreviated dtr)
YO 3 times, insert hook in petal indicated, YO and pull up a loop (5 loops on hook), (YO and draw through 2 loops on hook) 4 times.

PICOT
Ch 3, slip st in third ch from hook.

FLOWER

With Light Yellow, ch 5; join with slip st to form a ring.

Rnd 1 (Right side)**:** ★ Ch 6, working in back ridge of chs *(Fig. 1, page 94)*, sc in second ch from hook, dc in last 4 chs, slip st in ring **(petal made)**; repeat from ★ 5 times **more**; join with slip st in base of beginning ch-6, finish off.

Note: Loop a short piece of thread around any stitch to mark Rnd 1 as **right** side.

Rnd 2: With **right** side facing, holding first petal made towards you and working in **front** of petals, skip first slip st, join Yellow with slip st in ring **before** next slip st; ch 3 **(counts as first dc)**, (skip next slip st, dc in ring **before** next slip st) around; join with slip st to first dc, finish off.

Make as many Flowers as needed for desired length, working an odd number of Flowers.

BORDER
FIRST SIDE
Row 1 (Joining row)**:** With **right** side facing, join White with slip st in unworked ch at tip of any petal on any Flower; ch 8 (**counts as first dtr plus ch 3**), (sc in unworked ch at tip of next petal, ch 3) twice, ★ † overlapping tip of next petal in **front** of any petal tip on **next** Flower, working through both petals, tr in unworked ch at tip of petals †, ch 3, dc in unworked ch at tip of next petal, ch 3, repeat from † to † once, ch 3, (sc in unworked ch at tip of next petal, ch 3) twice; repeat from ★ across to fourth petal of last Flower, dtr in unworked ch at tip of fourth petal, leave remaining petals unworked.

Row 2: Ch 1, turn; sc in first dtr, ★ ch 3, skip next ch-3 sp, sc in next st; repeat from ★ across.

Row 3: Ch 1, turn; sc in first sc, ★ ch 3, sc in next ch-3 sp, ch 3, sc in next sc; repeat from ★ across; finish off.

SECOND SIDE
Row 1: With **wrong** side facing, join Green with sc in same ch at tip of same petal as first dtr made on Row 1 *(see Joining With Sc, page 94)*; ch 7, sc in unworked ch at tip of next petal, ch 5, sc in unworked ch at tip of next petal, ★ ch 1, sc in unworked ch at tip of next petal on next Flower, (ch 7, sc in unworked ch at tip of next petal) twice, ch 1, sc in unworked ch at tip of next petal on next Flower, ch 5, sc in unworked ch at tip of next petal; repeat from ★ across, ch 7, sc in unworked ch at tip of last petal (same petal as last dtr made on Row 1).

Row 2: Ch 1, turn; 9 sc in first ch-7 sp, (4 sc, work Picot, 4 sc) in next ch-5 sp, ★ sc in next ch-1 sp, 9 sc in next ch-7 sp, work Picot, 9 sc in next ch-7 sp, sc in next ch-1 sp, (4 sc, work Picot, 4 sc) in next ch-5 sp; repeat from ★ across to last ch-7 sp, 9 sc in last ch-7 sp, slip st in last sc; finish off.

57

SUNFLOWERS

Approxiate Width: 2³/₈" (6 cm)

ADDITIONAL SUPPLIES: Tapestry needle

SQUARE

With Brown, ch 4; join with slip st to form a ring.

Rnd 1 (Right side): Ch 3 (**counts as first dc**), 11 dc in ring; join with slip st to first dc, finish off: 12 dc.

Note: Loop a short piece of thread around any stitch to mark Rnd 1 as **right** side.

Rnd 2: With **right** side facing, join Yellow with slip st in any dc; ★ † ch 6, working in back ridge of chs *(Fig. 1, page 94)*, sc in second ch from hook, dc in last 4 chs (**petal made**) †, slip st in next dc on Rnd 1; repeat from ★ 10 times **more**, then repeat from † to † once; join with slip st to first slip st, finish off: 12 petals.

Rnd 3: With **right** side facing, join Green with sc in unworked ch at tip of any petal *(see Joining With Sc, page 94)*; ch 4, (sc in unworked ch at tip of next petal, ch 4) around; join with slip st to first sc: 12 ch-4 sps.

Rnd 4: Slip st in first ch-4 sp, ch 1, 3 sc in same sp and in next ch-4 sp, (3 dc, ch 2, 3 dc) in next ch-4 sp, ★ 3 sc in each of next 2 ch-4 sps, (3 dc, ch 2, 3 dc) in next ch-4 sp; repeat from ★ 2 times **more**; join with slip st to first sc, finish off.

Make as many Squares as needed for desired length less ½" (12 mm).

ASSEMBLY

Using photo as a guide, whipstitch Squares together with Green as follows:

Place two Squares with **wrong** sides together. Beginning in second ch of first corner ch-2, sew through both pieces once to secure the beginning of the seam, leaving an ample thread end to weave in later. Working through **inside** loops of each stitch on **both** pieces, insert the tapestry needle from **front** to **back** through first stitch and pull thread through *(Fig. A)*, ★ insert the needle from **front** to **back** through next stitch and pull thread through; repeat from ★ across ending in first ch of next corner ch-2.

BORDER

Rnd 1: With **right** side facing and holding strip vertically, join Green with sc in first corner ch-2 sp; 4 sc in same sp, sc in next 12 sts, 5 sc in next corner ch-2 sp, sc in next 12 sts, † (dc in next 2 sps, sc in next 12 sts) across to next corner ch-2 sp †, (5 sc in corner ch-2 sp, sc in next 12 sts) twice, repeat from † to † once; join with slip st to first sc, finish off.

Rnd 2: With **right** side facing, join White with sc in center sc of any corner 5-sc group; ch 3, sc in same st, skip next sc, ★ (sc, ch 3, sc) in next sc, skip next sc; repeat from ★ around; join with slip st to first sc, finish off.

Fig. A

VINTAGE FLOWERS

Approximate Width: 2 1/8" (5.5 cm)

STITCH GUIDE

TREBLE CROCHET *(abbreviated tr)*
YO twice, insert hook in sp indicated, YO and pull up a loop (4 loops on hook), (YO and draw through 2 loops on hook) 3 times.

DOUBLE TREBLE CROCHET *(abbreviated dtr)*
YO 3 times, insert hook in st or sp indicated, YO and pull up a loop (5 loops on hook), (YO and draw through 2 loops on hook) 4 times.

BEGINNING CLUSTER
Ch 2, ★ YO, insert hook in ring, YO and pull up a loop, YO and draw through 2 loops on hook; repeat from ★ once **more**, YO and draw through all 3 loops on hook.

CLUSTER
★ YO, insert hook in ring, YO and pull up a loop, YO and draw through 2 loops on hook; repeat from ★ 2 times **more**, YO and draw through all 4 loops on hook.

FLOWER

Ch 5; join with slip st to form a ring.

Rnd 1 (Right side)**:** Work beginning Cluster, (ch 3, work Cluster) 5 times, dc in top of beginning Cluster to form last ch-3 sp: 6 Clusters and 6 ch-3 sps.

Note: Loop a short piece of thread around any stitch to mark Rnd 1 as **right** side.

Rnd 2: Ch 1, (sc, ch 3) twice in last ch-3 sp made and in each ch-3 sp around; join with slip st to first sc, finish off.

Make as many Flowers as needed for desired length, allowing ½" (12 mm) between each Flower.

BORDER

Rnd 1 (Joining rnd): With **right** side of each Flower facing, join thread with slip st in any ch-3 sp on first Flower; ch 3 **(counts as first dc)**, 2 dc in same sp, hdc in next ch-3 sp, 2 hdc in next ch-3 sp, (3 dc, ch 2, 3 dc) in next ch-3 sp, 2 hdc in next ch-3 sp, hdc in next ch-3 sp, 3 dc in next ch-3 sp, ★ 3 dc in any ch-3 sp on **next** Flower, hdc in next ch-3 sp, 2 hdc in next ch-3 sp, (3 dc, ch 2, 3 dc) in next ch-3 sp, 2 hdc in next ch-3 sp, hdc in next ch-3 sp, 3 dc in next ch-3 sp; repeat from ★ across, ch 7, tr in next ch-3 sp, ch 2, dc in next ch-3 sp, ch 2, sc in next ch-3 sp, ch 2, dc in next ch-3 sp, ch 2, tr in next ch-3 sp, ch 2, † (dtr around post of next dc, ch 2) twice, tr in next ch-3 sp, ch 2, dc in next ch-3 sp, ch 2, sc in next ch-3 sp, ch 2, dc in next ch-3 sp, ch 2, tr in next ch-3 sp, ch 2 †; repeat from † to † across, dtr in first dc to form last sp.

Rnd 2: Ch 1, **turn**; sc in last dtr made, ch 2, ★ skip next ch-2 sp, sc in next st, ch 2; repeat from ★ across to next ch-7 sp, skip next 2 chs, sc in next ch, leave remaining sts unworked.

Rnd 3: Turn; slip st in first ch-2 sp, ch 1, (sc, ch 3, sc) in same sp and in each ch-2 sp across, ch 3, (sc, ch 3) twice around post of next dtr, skip next dc, ★ † (sc in next st, ch 3, skip next st) 4 times, (sc, ch 3) twice in next ch-2 sp, skip next dc †, sc in next dc, (ch 3, skip next st, sc in next st) 3 times, skip next 2 dc; repeat from ★ across to last Flower, then repeat from † to † once, (sc in next st, ch 3, skip next st) 4 times, (sc, ch 3) twice in last sp; join with slip st to first sc, finish off.

PETUNIAS

Approximate Width: 1¹⁄₈" (2.75 cm)

STITCH GUIDE

TREBLE CROCHET *(abbreviated tr)*
YO twice, insert hook in sp indicated, YO and pull up a loop (4 loops on hook), (YO and draw through 2 loops on hook) 3 times.

FLOWER
Ch 3, dc in same sp, (ch 3, slip st in top of dc just made, dc in same sp on Foundation Row) 7 times, drop loop from hook, working **behind** 8-dc group just made, insert hook in top of beginning ch-3 of Flower, hook dropped loop and draw through st.

LEAF
Ch 3, tr in sp indicated, ch 3, sc in top of tr just made, ch 3, slip st in same sp on Foundation Row.

INSTRUCTIONS

Foundation Row: With White, ★ ch 4, dc in fourth ch from hook; repeat from ★ an even number of times for desired length: an odd number of dc worked.

Row 1 (Right side)**:** Ch 7, dc in fourth ch from hook and around post of first dc on Foundation Row, ★ dc around post of next dc on Foundation Row, ch 4, dc in fourth ch from hook and around post of same dc on Foundation Row; repeat from ★ across; finish off.

Note: Loop a short piece of thread around any stitch to mark Row 1 as **right** side.

Row 2: With **wrong** side facing and working in unworked sps on Foundation Row, join Pink with slip st in second sp on Foundation Row; work Flower, ★ ch 7, skip next sp, slip st in next sp, work Flower; repeat from ★ across to last sp, leave last sp unworked; finish off.

Row 3: With **right** side facing, join Green with slip st in first unworked sp on Foundation Row; (work Leaf in same sp) twice, ch 3, ★ working **behind** Flowers, skip next Flower, working **around** next ch-7, slip st in unworked sp on Foundation Row, (work Leaf in same sp) twice, ch 3; repeat from ★ across to last sp on Foundation Row, slip st in last sp, (work Leaf in same sp) twice; finish off.

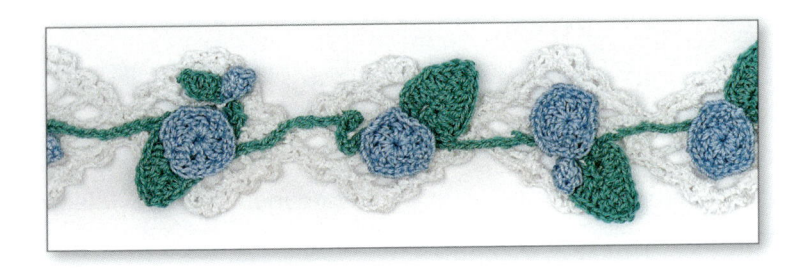

MORNING GLORIES

Approximate Width: 2" (5 cm)

ADDITIONAL SUPPLIES: Tapestry needle

TRELLIS

Row 1 (Wrong side): With White, ch 17, dc in eighth ch from hook, place marker around skipped chs for st placement, ★ ch 2, skip next 2 chs, dc in next ch; repeat from ★ across: 4 sps.

Note: Loop a short piece of thread around the **back** of any stitch on Row 1 to mark **right** side.

Row 2: Ch 5 (**counts as first dc plus ch 2, now and throughout**), turn; (dc in next dc, ch 2) 3 times, skip next 2 chs, dc in next ch.

Rows 3 and 4: Ch 5, turn; dc in next dc, (ch 2, dc in next dc) across.

Row 5: Ch 16, turn; dc in eighth ch from hook, ch 2, skip next 2 chs, ★ dc in next ch, ch 2, skip next 2 chs; repeat from ★ once **more**, dc in last dc on previous row.

Repeat Rows 2-5 as many times as needed for desired length, ending by working Row 4; do **not** finish off.

BORDER

Rnd 1: Do **not** turn; slip st around post of first dc, ch 1, (sc, ch 3, sc) in same sp and in next 2 sps, † sc in next sp, (ch 3, sc in same sp) 3 times, (sc, ch 3, sc) in next 2 sps, sc in next 2 sps, (sc, ch 3, sc) in next 2 sps †; repeat from † to † across to marker, remove marker, ★ sc in next sp, (ch 3, sc in same sp) 3 times, (sc, ch 3, sc) in next 2 sps; repeat from ★ 2 times **more**, [sc in next 2 sps, (sc, ch 3, sc) in next 2 sps, sc in next sp, (ch 3, sc in same sp) 3 times, (sc, ch 3, sc) in next 2 sps] across, (sc in same sp as first sc, ch 3) twice; join with slip st to first sc, finish off.

FINISHING
FLOWER
With Blue, ch 4; join with slip st to form a ring.

Rnd 1 (Right side)**:** Ch 3 (**counts as first dc**), dc in ring, ch 1, (2 dc in ring, ch 1) 4 times; join with slip st to first dc: 10 dc.

Rnd 2: Ch 1, sc in same st and in next dc, ch 3, (sc in next 2 dc, ch 3) around; join with slip st to first sc, finish off leaving a long end for sewing.

Make as many Flowers as desired.

BUD
With Blue, ch 4, 5 dc in fourth ch from hook (**3 skipped chs count as first dc**), drop loop from hook, insert hook in first dc, hook dropped loop and pull through st; finish off leaving a long end for sewing.

Make as many Buds as desired.

SMALL LEAF
Row 1 (Right side)**:** With Green, ch 4, sc in second ch from hook, hdc in next ch, (dc, ch 2, slip st) in last ch; finish off leaving a long end for sewing.

Make as many Small Leaves as desired.

LARGE LEAF & STEM
Row 1 (Right side)**:** With Green, ch 6, sc in second ch from hook and in each ch across, ch 3, **turn**; 3 dc in first sc, dc in next 2 sc, hdc in next sc, 3 sc in last sc; working in free loops of beginning ch *(Fig. 2, page 94)*, skip first ch, hdc in next ch, dc in next 2 chs, (3 dc, ch 2, slip st) in last ch; do **not** finish off.

Using photo as a guide, make a ch of desired length for Stem; finish off leaving a long end for sewing.

Make as many Large Leaves as desired, with or without Stems.

ASSEMBLY
Using photo as a guide, page 64, sew Flowers, Buds, Leaves and Stems to Trellis as desired.

65

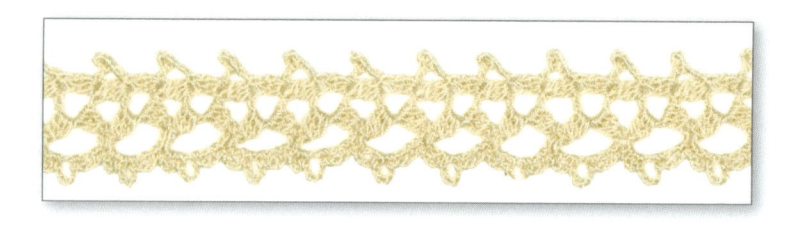

WISPY LACE

Approximate Width: 1¼" (3.25 cm)

STITCH GUIDE

CLUSTER (uses one st or sp)
★ YO, insert hook in st or sp indicated, YO and pull up a loop, YO and draw through 2 loops on hook; repeat from ★ 2 times **more**, YO and draw through all 4 loops on hook, ch 1 to close.

INSTRUCTIONS

Foundation Row: Ch 8, work Cluster in eighth ch from hook, ★ ch 6, **turn**; sc in fourth ch from hook, ch 2, work Cluster in Cluster, ch 7, **turn**; work Cluster in Cluster; repeat from ★ for desired length.

Row 1 (Right side)**:** Turn; slip st in first ch-7 sp, ch 3, ★ YO, insert hook in same sp, YO and pull up a loop, YO and draw through 2 loops on hook; repeat from ★ once **more**, YO and draw through all 3 loops on hook, ch 8, work Cluster in same sp, work (Cluster, ch 8, Cluster) in each ch-7 sp across.

Row 2: Ch 1, turn; (sc, ch 3, sc, ch 5, sc, ch 3, sc) in each ch-8 sp across; finish off.

POINSETTIAS

Approximate Width: 2" (5 cm)

STITCH GUIDE
TREBLE CROCHET
(abbreviated tr)
YO twice, insert hook in st indicated, YO and pull up a loop (4 loops on hook), (YO and draw through 2 loops on hook) 3 times.

FIRST MOTIF

With Yellow, ch 4; join with slip st to form a ring.

Rnd 1 (Right side)**:** Ch 2 **(counts as first hdc)**, 11 hdc in ring; join with slip st to first hdc, finish off: 12 hdc.

Note: Loop a short piece of thread around any stitch to mark Rnd 1 as **right** side.

Rnd 2: With **right** side facing, join Red with slip st in any hdc; ch 7, working in back ridge of chs *(Fig. 1, page 94)*, sc in second ch from hook, dc in next ch, tr in last 4 chs **(petal made)**, skip next hdc, ★ slip st in next hdc, ch 7, working in back ridge of chs, sc in second ch from hook, dc in next ch, tr in last 4 chs **(petal made)**, skip next hdc; repeat from ★ around; join with slip st to first slip st, finish off: 6 petals.

67

Rnd 3: With **right** side facing, working **behind** petals and in skipped hdc on Rnd 1, join Green with slip st in any skipped hdc; ch 7 **(counts as first tr plus ch 3)**, (tr, ch 3) twice in next 5 skipped hdc, tr in same st as first tr, ch 1, hdc in first tr to form last ch-3 sp: 12 ch-3 sps.

Rnd 4: Ch 1, insert hook in unworked ch at tip of nearest petal **and** in last ch-3 sp made, YO and pull up a loop, YO and draw through both loops on hook **(sc made)**, ch 3, ★ (sc, ch 3) twice in next ch-3 sp, insert hook in unworked ch at tip of next petal **and** in next ch-3 sp, YO and pull up a loop, YO and draw through both loops on hook **(sc made)**, ch 3; repeat from ★ 4 times **more**, (sc, ch 3, sc) in last ch-3 sp, place marker around ch-3 just made for joining placement, ch 3; join with slip st to first sc, finish off.

ADDITIONAL MOTIFS

Work same as First Motif through Rnd 3: 12 ch-3 sps.

Rnd 4 (Joining rnd)**:** Ch 1, insert hook in unworked ch at tip of nearest petal **and** in last ch-3 sp made, YO and pull up a loop, YO and draw through both loops on hook **(sc made)**, ch 3, ★ † (sc, ch 3) twice in next ch-3 sp, insert hook in unworked ch at tip of next petal **and** in next ch-3 sp, YO and pull up a loop, YO and draw through both loops on hook **(sc made)**, ch 3 †; repeat from ★ once **more**, (sc, ch 3, sc) in next ch-3 sp, place marker around ch-3 just made for joining placement, ch 3, insert hook in unworked ch at tip of next petal **and** in next ch-3 sp, YO and pull up a loop, YO and draw through both loops on hook **(sc made)**, ch 3, repeat from † to † once, sc in next ch-3 sp, ch 1; holding Motifs with **wrong** sides together, sc in marked ch-3 sp on **previous Motif**, ch 1, sc in same sp on **new Motif**, ch 3, insert hook in unworked ch at tip of next petal **and** in next ch-3 sp, YO and pull up a loop, YO and draw through both loops on hook **(sc made)**, ch 3, sc in next ch-3 sp, ch 1, skip next 2 ch-3 sps on **previous Motif**, sc in next ch-3 sp, ch 1, sc in same sp on **new Motif**, ch 3; join with slip st to first sc, finish off.

Make as many Additional Motifs as needed for desired length less 2¼" (5.75 cm).

LAST MOTIF
Work same as First Motif through Rnd 3: 12 ch-3 sps.

Rnd 4 (Joining rnd)**:** Ch 1, insert hook in unworked ch at tip of nearest petal **and** in last ch-3 sp made, YO and pull up a loop, YO and draw through both loops on hook **(sc made)**, ch 3, ★ (sc, ch 3) twice in next ch-3 sp, insert hook in unworked ch at tip of next petal **and** in next ch-3 sp, YO and pull up a loop, YO and draw through both loops on hook **(sc made)**, ch 3; repeat from ★ 3 times **more**, sc in next ch-3 sp, ch 1; holding Motifs with **wrong** sides together, sc in marked ch-3 sp on **previous Motif**, ch 1, sc in same sp on **new Motif**, ch 3, insert hook in unworked ch at tip of next petal **and** in next ch-3 sp, YO and pull up a loop, YO and draw through both loops on hook **(sc made)**, ch 3, sc in next ch-3 sp, ch 1, skip next 2 ch-3 sps on **previous Motif**, sc in next ch-3 sp, ch 1, sc in same sp on **new Motif**, ch 3; join with slip st to first sc, finish off.

BORDER
With **right** side facing, join White with sc in any ch-3 sp *(see Joining With Sc, page 94)*; (sc, ch 3, 2 sc) in same sp, (2 sc, ch 3, 2 sc) in each ch-3 sp around; join with slip st to first sc, finish off.

BACHELOR BUTTONS

Approximate Width: 2" (5 cm)

STITCH GUIDE
TREBLE CROCHET
   (abbreviated tr)
YO twice, insert hook in st or sp indicated, YO and pull up a loop (4 loops on hook), (YO and draw through 2 loops on hook) 3 times.
BEGINNING CLUSTER
   (uses one sp)
Ch 3, ★ YO twice, insert hook in sp indicated, YO and pull up a loop, (YO and draw through 2 loops on hook) twice; repeat from ★ once **more**, YO and draw through all 3 loops on hook.
CLUSTER *(uses one sp)*
★ YO twice, insert hook in sp indicated, YO and pull up a loop, (YO and draw through 2 loops on hook) twice; repeat from ★ 2 times **more**, YO and draw through all 4 loops on hook.

FLOWER
With Blue, ch 4; join with slip st to form a ring.

Rnd 1 (Right side)**:** Ch 1, (sc in ring, ch 5) 6 times; join with slip st to first sc: 6 ch-5 sps.

Note: Loop a short piece of thread around any stitch to mark Rnd 1 as **right** side.

Rnd 2: (Slip st, ch 1, sc) in first ch-5 sp, (ch 4, sc in same sp) 5 times (**petal made**), ★ sc in next ch-5 sp, (ch 4, sc in same sp) 5 times; repeat from ★ around; do **not** join: 6 petals.

Rnd 3: Working **behind** petals and in unworked sc on Rnd 1, sc in first sc, ch 5, (sc in next sc, ch 5) around; join with slip st to first sc, finish off.

Make as many additional Flowers as needed for desired length, allowing approximately ¾" (19 mm) between each Flower.

LEAVES

Joining Row: With **right** side facing, join Green with slip st in any ch-5 sp on any Flower; work (beginning Cluster, ch 5, Cluster) in same sp, place marker around last ch-5 made for Border placement, ch 5, (sc in next ch-5 sp, ch 5) twice, ★ work (Cluster, ch 5, Cluster) in next ch-5 sp on same Flower, (work Cluster, ch 5) twice in any ch-5 sp on next Flower, (sc in next ch-5 sp, ch 5) twice; repeat from ★ across to last 3 ch-5 sps on last Flower, work (Cluster, ch 5, Cluster) in next ch-5 sp, leave remaining ch-5 sps unworked; finish off.

BORDER

Rnd 1: With **right** side facing, join White with sc in marked ch-5 sp on Leaves *(see Joining With Sc, page 94)*; (4 sc, ch 5, 5 sc) in same sp, ★ (5 sc, ch 5, 5 sc) in next 3 ch-5 sps, sc in next 2 ch-5 sps; repeat from ★ across to last 4 ch-5 sps, (5 sc, ch 5, 5 sc) in last 4 ch-5 sps, ch 5 **(counts as tr plus ch 1)**, (tr, ch 1, tr) in next Cluster, ch 3, (dc in next unworked ch-5 sp on Flower, ch 3) twice, † skip next Cluster, tr in sp **before** next Cluster *(Fig. 3, page 95)*, (ch 1, tr in same sp) 4 times, ch 3, (dc in next unworked ch-5 sp on Flower, ch 3) twice †; repeat from † to † across to last Cluster, (tr, ch 1) twice in last Cluster, tr in first sc to join.

Begin working in rows.

Row 1: Ch 1, turn; sc in first tr, ch 5, skip next tr, sc in next tr, ch 5, (sc in next dc, ch 5) twice, ★ sc in next tr, ch 5, (skip next tr, sc in next tr, ch 5) twice, (sc in next dc, ch 5) twice; repeat from ★ across to last 3 tr, sc in next tr, ch 2, skip next tr, dc in last tr to form last ch-5 sp, leave remaining sts unworked.

Row 2: Ch 1, turn; (sc, ch 5, sc) in last ch-5 sp made and in each ch-5 sp across; finish off.

FUCHSIAS

Approximate Width: 1½" (3.75 cm)

STITCH GUIDE
CLUSTER
★ YO 3 times, insert hook in ring, YO and pull up a loop, (YO and draw through 2 loops on hook) 3 times; repeat from ★ once **more**, YO and draw through all 3 loops on hook.
PICOT
Ch 3, slip st in top of last st made.

FLOWERS
With Lt Purple, ch 6; join with slip st to form a ring.

Row 1 (Right side): Ch 5, work (Cluster, Picot, ch 5, sc) in ring **(petal made)**, (ch 3, sc in ring) 3 times, ch 5, work (Cluster, Picot, ch 5, slip st) in ring **(petal made)**, ★ ch 17, slip st in sixth ch from hook to form next ring, ch 5, work (Cluster, Picot, ch 5, sc) in ring, (ch 3, sc in ring) 3 times, ch 5, work (Cluster, Picot, ch 5, slip st) in ring; repeat from ★ until desired length is reached; finish off.

Note: Loop a short piece of thread around any stitch to mark Row 1 as **right** side.

Row 2: With **right** side facing, join Purple with sc in ring **before** first petal made *(see Joining With Sc, page 94)*; ch 2, working **behind** petals, (slip st, ch 3, dc, work Picot, ch 3, slip st) in next 3 ch-3 sps, ch 2, skip next petal, sc in same ring, ★ ch 3, skip next 5 chs, sc in next ch, ch 3, sc in ring **before** next petal, ch 2, (slip st, ch 3, dc, work Picot, ch 3, slip st) in next 3 ch-3 sps, ch 2, skip next petal, sc in same ring; repeat from ★ across; finish off.

BORDER

Row 1: With **right** side facing and holding petals towards you, join Ecru with sc in last sc made; dc in ring, (ch 2, dc in same ring) 4 times, working **around** Row 1, sc in next sc on Row 2, ★ dc in free loop of same ch as next sc on Row 2 *(Fig. 2, page 94)*, (ch 2, dc in same st) twice, working **around** Row 1, sc in next sc on Row 2, dc in next ring, (ch 2, dc in same ring) 4 times, working **around** Row 1, sc in next sc on Row 2; repeat from ★ across.

Row 2: Ch 1, turn; (sc, ch 3, sc) in first 4 ch-2 sps, ★ skip next ch-2 sp, (sc, ch 3, sc) in next dc, skip next ch-2 sp, (sc, ch 3, sc) in next 4 ch-2 sps; repeat from ★ across to last sc, slip st in last sc; finish off.

IRISH ROSES

Approximate Width: 2½" (6.25 cm)

FIRST MOTIF

Ch 5; join with slip st to form a ring.

Rnd 1 (Right side): Ch 1, sc in ring, (ch 3, sc in ring) 5 times, dc in first sc to form last ch-3 sp: 6 ch-3 sps.

Note: Loop a short piece of thread around any stitch to mark Rnd 1 as **right** side.

Rnd 2: Ch 1, (sc, 5 dc, sc) in last ch-3 sp made **(petal made)** and in each ch-3 sp around; join with slip st to first sc: 6 petals.

Rnd 3: Ch 1, sc in sp **before** first sc *(Fig. 3, page 95)*, ★ ch 4, working **behind** petal, skip next 7 sts, sc in sp **before** next sc; repeat from ★ around, ch 3, working **behind** last petal, sc in first sc to form last ch-4 sp: 6 ch-4 sps.

Rnd 4: Ch 3 **(counts as first dc)**, (dc, sc) in last ch-4 sp made, (sc, 7 dc, sc) in next 5 ch-4 sps, (sc, 5 dc) in same sp as first dc; join with slip st to first dc: 6 petals.

Rnd 5: Ch 1, sc in same st, ch 3, skip next 4 sts, sc in next dc, ★ ch 3, (skip next dc, sc in next dc, ch 3) twice, skip next 4 sts, sc in next dc; repeat from ★ 4 times **more**, ch 3, skip next dc, sc in next dc, ch 3, skip last dc; join with slip st to first sc, place marker around last ch-3 made for joining placement, finish off.

ADDITIONAL MOTIFS

Work same as First Motif through Rnd 4: 6 petals.

Rnd 5 (Joining rnd): Ch 1, sc in same st, † ch 3, skip next 4 sts, sc in next dc, (ch 3, skip next dc, sc in next dc) twice †; repeat from † to † 2 times **more**, place marker around last ch-3 made for joining placement, repeat from † to † twice, ch 3, skip next 4 sts, sc in next dc, ch 1; holding Motifs with **wrong** sides together, sc in marked ch-3 sp on **previous Motif**, ch 1, skip next dc on **new Motif**, sc in next dc, ch 1, sc in next ch-3 sp on **previous Motif**, ch 1, skip last dc on **new Motif**; join with slip st to first sc, finish off.

Make as many Additional Motifs as needed for desired length less 2¾" (7 cm).

LAST MOTIF

Work same as First Motif through Rnd 4: 6 petals.

Rnd 5 (Joining rnd)**:** Ch 1, sc in same st, ch 3, skip next 4 sts, sc in next dc, ★ ch 3, (skip next dc, sc in next dc, ch 3) twice, skip next 4 sts, sc in next dc; repeat from ★ 4 times **more**, ch 1; holding Motifs with **wrong** sides together, sc in marked ch-3 sp on **previous Motif**, ch 1, skip next dc on **new Motif**, sc in next dc, ch 1, sc in next ch-3 sp on **previous Motif**, ch 1, skip last dc on **new Motif**; join with slip st to first sc, do **not** finish off.

BORDER

Rnd 1: Slip st in first ch-3 sp, ch 1, 4 sc in same sp and in each of next 15 ch-3 sps, skip next joining, † (4 sc in each of next 7 ch-3 sps, skip next joining) across to last Motif †, 4 sc in each of next 16 ch-3 sps, skip next joining, repeat from † to † once; join with slip st to first sc.

Rnd 2: Slip st in next 2 sc, ch 1, sc in same st and in next 59 sc, skip next 4 sc, (sc in next 24 sc, skip next 4 sc) across to last Motif, sc in next 60 sc, skip next 4 sc, (sc in next 24 sc, skip next 4 sc) across; join with slip st to first sc.

Rnd 3: Slip st in next 2 sc, ch 1, sc in same st, † (ch 3, skip next sc, sc in next sc) 27 times, skip next 5 sc, ★ sc in next sc, (ch 3, skip next sc, sc in next sc) 9 times, skip next 5 sc; repeat from ★ across to last Motif †, sc in next sc, repeat from † to † once; join with slip st to first sc, finish off.

SPRING BEAUTY

STITCH GUIDE

2-TR CLUSTER (uses one st)
★ YO twice, insert hook in st indicated, YO and pull up a loop, (YO and draw through 2 loops on hook) twice; repeat from ★ once **more**, YO and draw through all 3 loops on hook.

3-TR CLUSTER (uses one st)
★ YO twice, insert hook in st indicated, YO and pull up a loop, (YO and draw through 2 loops on hook) twice; repeat from ★ 2 times **more**, YO and draw through all 4 loops on hook.

INSTRUCTIONS

Foundation Row (Right side)**:**
★ Ch 5, work 2-tr Cluster in fifth ch from hook; repeat from ★ until within ½" (12 mm) of desired length, working an even number of 2-tr Clusters; do **not** finish off.

Approximate Width: 1¾" (4.5 cm)

Begin working in rounds.

Rnd 1: Ch 5; working across long edge of Foundation Row, † ★ (work 3-tr Cluster, ch 5) twice in ch at base of next 2-tr Cluster, sc in ch at base of next 2-tr Cluster, ch 5; repeat from ★ across to last 2 2-tr Clusters, work (3-tr Cluster, ch 5, 3-tr Cluster) in ch at base of next 2-tr Cluster, place marker around last ch-5 made for st placement, ch 5 †, sc in ch at base of last 2-tr Cluster, ch 5; working across opposite side of Foundation Row, repeat from † to † once; join with slip st to top of last 2-tr Cluster.

Rnd 2: (Slip st, ch 1, sc) in first ch-5 sp, (ch 3, sc in same sp) 3 times, sc in next ch-5 sp, (ch 3, sc in same sp) 3 times, (sc, ch 3, sc) in next 2 ch-5 sps, † sc in next ch-5 sp, (ch 3, sc in same sp) 3 times, (sc, ch 3, sc) in next 2 ch-5 sps †; repeat from † to † across to next marker, ★ sc in next ch-5 sp, (ch 3, sc in same sp) 3 times; repeat from ★ 3 times **more**, (sc, ch 3, sc) in next 2 ch-5 sps, repeat from † to † across to next marker, [sc in next ch-5 sp, (ch 3, sc in same sp) 3 times] twice; join with slip st to first sc, finish off.

CHRYSANTHEMUMS

Approximate Width: 2³/₈" (6 cm)

ADDITIONAL SUPPLIES: ¼" (6 mm) wide ribbon - desired length

STITCH GUIDE

TREBLE CROCHET (abbreviated tr)
YO twice, insert hook in sp indicated, YO and pull up a loop (4 loops on hook), (YO and draw through 2 loops on hook) 3 times.

BEGINNING CLUSTER (uses last ch-3 sp made)
Ch 3, ★ YO twice, insert hook in last ch-3 sp made, (YO and pull up a loop, YO and draw through 2 loops on hook) twice; repeat from ★ 2 times **more**, YO and draw through all 4 loops on hook.

CLUSTER (uses one sp)
★ YO twice, insert hook in sp indicated, (YO and pull up a loop, YO and draw through 2 loops on hook) twice; repeat from ★ 3 times **more**, YO and draw through all 5 loops on hook.

FIRST FLOWER

Ch 6; join with slip st to form a ring.

Rnd 1 (Right side)**:** Ch 1, sc in ring, (ch 3, sc in ring) 7 times, dc in first sc to form last ch-3 sp: 8 ch-3 sps.

Note: Loop a short piece of thread around any stitch to mark Rnd 1 as **right** side.

Rnd 2: Work beginning Cluster, (ch 4, work Cluster in next ch-3 sp) around, ch 3, sc in top of beginning Cluster to form last ch-4 sp.

Rnd 3: Ch 1, sc in last ch-4 sp made, ch 5, (sc, ch 5) twice in next 3 ch-3 sps, place marker around last ch-5 made for joining placement, (sc, ch 5) twice in next 4 ch-3 sps, sc in same sp as first sc, ch 5; join with slip st to first sc, finish off, place marker around last ch-5 made for Border placement: 16 ch-5 sps.

ADDITIONAL FLOWERS

Work same as First Flower through Rnd 2: 8 ch-4 sps.

Rnd 3 (Joining rnd)**:** Ch 1, sc in last ch-4 sp made, ch 5, (sc, ch 5) twice in next 3 ch-3 sps, place marker around last ch-5 made for joining placement, (sc, ch 5) twice in next 2 ch-3 sps, (sc, ch 5, sc) in next ch-3 sp, ch 2; holding Flowers with **wrong** sides together, sc in marked ch-5 sp on **previous Flower**, ch 2, sc in next ch-3 sp on **new Flower**, ch 2, sc in next ch-5 sp on **previous Flower**, ch 2, sc in same sp on **new Flower**, ch 2, sc in next ch-5 sp on **previous Flower**, ch 2, sc in same sp as first sc on **new Flower**, ch 5; join with slip st to first sc, finish off: 16 ch-5 sps.

Make as many Additional Flowers as needed for desired length less 2" (5 cm).

LAST FLOWER

Work same as First Flower through Rnd 2: 8 ch-4 sps.

Rnd 3 (Joining rnd)**:** Ch 1, sc in last ch-4 sp made, ch 5, (sc, ch 5) twice in next 5 ch-3 sps, (sc, ch 5, sc) in next ch-3 sp, ch 2; holding Flowers with **wrong** sides together, sc in marked ch-5 sp on **previous Flower**, ch 2, sc in next ch-3 sp on **new Flower**, ch 2, sc in next ch-5 sp on **previous Flower**, ch 2, sc in same sp on **new Flower**, ch 2, sc in next ch-5 sp on **previous Flower**, ch 2, sc in same sp as first sc on **new Flower**, ch 5; join with slip st to first sc, finish off.

BORDER

Row 1: With **right** side facing, join thread with slip st in marked ch-5 sp on First Flower; ch 7 **(counts as first tr plus ch 3)**, dc in next ch-5 sp, ch 3, sc in next ch-5 sp, ch 3, dc in next ch-5 sp, ch 3, tr in next ch-5 sp, ★ ch 3, skip next joining, tr in next ch-5 sp, ch 3, dc in next ch-5 sp, ch 3, sc in next ch-5 sp, ch 3, dc in next ch-5 sp, ch 3, tr in next ch-5 sp; repeat from ★ across to last 8 ch-5 sps on Last Flower, leave remaining ch-5 sps unworked.

Row 2 (Eyelet row)**:** Ch 6 **(counts as first dc plus ch 3)**, turn; skip first ch-3 sp, dc in next dc, ★ ch 3, skip next ch-3 sp, dc in next st; repeat from ★ across.

Row 3: Ch 1, turn; sc in first dc, (3 sc in next ch-3 sp, sc in next dc) across; finish off.

Weave ribbon through Eyelet row.

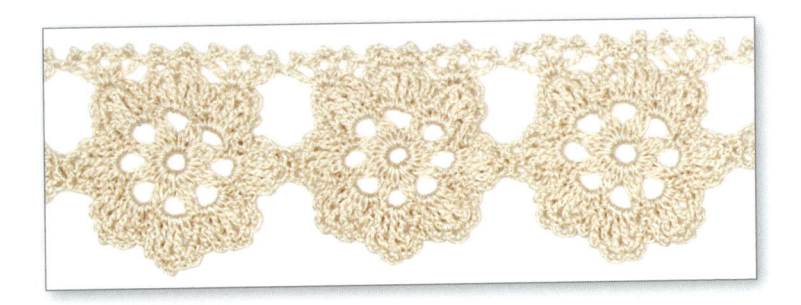

ANTIQUE BLOSSOMS

Approximate Width: 2½" (6.25 cm)

STITCH GUIDE

TREBLE CROCHET *(abbreviated tr)*
YO twice, insert hook in st or sp indicated, YO and pull up a loop (4 loops on hook), (YO and draw through 2 loops on hook) 3 times.

DOUBLE TREBLE CROCHET *(abbreviated dtr)*
YO 3 times, insert hook in sp indicated, YO and pull up a loop (5 loops on hook), (YO and draw through 2 loops on hook) 4 times.

BEGINNING CLUSTER
Ch 2, ★ YO, insert hook in ring, YO and pull up a loop, YO and draw through 2 loops on hook; repeat from ★ once **more**, YO and draw through all 3 loops on hook.

CLUSTER
★ YO, insert hook in ring, YO and pull up a loop, YO and draw through 2 loops on hook; repeat from ★ 2 times **more**, YO and draw through all 4 loops on hook.

PICOT
Ch 3, sc in third ch from hook.

FIRST MOTIF

Ch 8; join with slip st to form a ring.

Rnd 1 (Right side)**:** Work beginning Cluster, (ch 5, work Cluster) 7 times, ch 1, tr in top of beginning Cluster to form last ch-5 sp: 8 ch-5 sps.

Note: Loop a short piece of thread around any stitch to mark Rnd 1 as **right** side.

Rnd 2: Ch 1, work **[**sc, ch 1, dc, ch 1, (tr, ch 1) twice, dc, ch 1, sc**]** in last ch-5 sp made and in each ch-5 sp around; join with slip st to first sc: 40 ch-1 sps.

Rnd 3: (Slip st, ch 1, sc) in first ch-1 sp, ch 3, place marker around ch-3 just made for Border placement, † (sc in next ch-1 sp, ch 3) 3 times, sc in next 2 ch-1 sps, ch 3 †; repeat from † to † 2 times **more**, (sc in next ch-1 sp, ch 3) twice, place marker around last ch-3 made for joining placement, sc in next ch-1 sp, ch 3, ★ sc in next 2 ch-1 sps, ch 3, (sc in next ch-1 sp, ch 3) 3 times; repeat from ★ 3 times **more**, sc in last ch-1 sp; join with slip st to first sc, finish off.

ADDITIONAL MOTIFS

Work same as First Motif through Rnd 2: 40 ch-1 sps.

Rnd 3 (Joining rnd)**:** (Slip st, ch 1, sc) in first ch-1 sp, † ch 3, (sc in next ch-1 sp, ch 3) 3 times, sc in next 2 ch-1 sps †; repeat from † to † 2 times **more**, (ch 3, sc in next ch-1 sp) 3 times, place marker around last ch-3 made for joining placement, sc in next ch-1 sp, ch 3, sc in next 2 ch-1 sps, repeat from † to † 3 times, ch 3, sc in next ch-1 sp, ch 1; holding Motifs with **wrong** sides together, slip st in marked ch-3 sp on **previous Motif**, ch 1, sc in next ch-1 sp on **new Motif**, ch 1, slip st in next ch-3 sp on **previous Motif**, ch 1, sc in next ch-1 sp on **new Motif**, ch 3, sc in last ch-1 sp; join with slip st to first sc, finish off.

Make as many Additional Motifs as needed for desired length less 2½" (6.25 cm).

LAST MOTIF

Work same as First Motif through Rnd 2: 40 ch-1 sps.

Rnd 3 (Joining rnd)**:** (Slip st, ch 1, sc) in first ch-1 sp, ch 3, ★ (sc in next ch-1 sp, ch 3) 3 times, sc in next 2 ch-1 sps, ch 3; repeat from ★ 6 times **more**, sc in next ch-1 sp, ch 1; holding Motifs with **wrong** sides together, slip st in marked ch-3 sp on **previous Motif**, ch 1, sc in next ch-1 sp on **new Motif**, ch 1, slip st in next ch-3 sp on **previous Motif**, ch 1, sc in next ch-1 sp on **new Motif**, ch 3, sc in last ch-1 sp; join with slip st to first sc, finish off.

BORDER

With **right** side facing, join thread with slip st in marked ch-3 sp on First Motif; ch 6, skip next ch-3 sp, tr in next ch-3 sp, (work Picot, tr in same sp) 3 times, skip next 2 ch-3 sps, (sc, work Picot, sc) in next 2 ch-3 sps, skip next 2 ch-3 sps, tr in next ch-3 sp, (work Picot, tr in same sp) 3 times, ★ skip next 3 ch-3 sps on **next** Motif, tr in next ch-3 sp, (work Picot, tr in same sp) 3 times, skip next 2 ch-3 sps, (sc, work Picot, sc) in next 2 ch-3 sps, skip next 2 ch-3 sps, tr in next ch-3 sp, (work Picot, tr in same sp) 3 times; repeat from ★ across, ch 1, skip next ch-3 sp, dtr in next ch-3 sp, leave remaining sps unworked; finish off.

COSMOS

Approximate Width: 1½" (3.75 cm)

STITCH GUIDE

DOUBLE TREBLE CROCHET *(abbreviated dtr)*
YO 3 times, insert hook in sp indicated, YO and pull up a loop (5 loops on hook), (YO and draw through 2 loops on hook) 4 times.

LEAF
Ch 8, slip st in fourth ch from hook, ch 3, skip next 3 chs, slip st in last ch.

Note: Loop a short piece of thread around any stitch to mark Rnd 1 as **right** side.

Rnd 2: Ch 3 (**counts as first dc, now and throughout**), dc in last ch-3 sp made, ★ † (ch 1, dc in same sp) 4 times, ch 3, slip st in same sp (**petal made**) †, (slip st, ch 3, dc) in next ch-3 sp; repeat from ★ 4 times **more**, then repeat from † to † once; do **not** join: 6 petals.

FIRST MOTIF

With Blue, ch 5; join with slip st to form a ring.

Rnd 1 (Right side)**:** Ch 1, sc in ring, (ch 3, sc in ring) 5 times, dc in first sc to form last ch-3 sp: 6 ch-3 sps.

Rnd 3: Working **behind** petals and in unworked sc on Rnd 1, (slip st, ch 1, sc) in first sc, ch 4, (sc in next sc, ch 4) around; join with slip st to first sc, finish off: 6 ch-4 sps.

83

Rnd 4: With **right** side facing, join White with sc in any ch-4 sp *(see Joining With Sc, page 94)*; † ch 10, slip st in fourth ch from hook, ch 3, skip next 3 chs, slip st in next ch (**first Leaf made**), work Leaf 3 times, ch 6, slip st in fourth ch from hook, ch 1, skip next ch, slip st in last ch (**joining Leaf made**), work Leaf, skip joining Leaf, slip st in base of next Leaf, (work Leaf, slip st in base of next Leaf) 3 times, slip st in next ch, ch 1, (sc in next ch-4 sp, ch 5) twice †, sc in next ch-4 sp, repeat from † to † once; join with slip st to first sc, finish off.

ADDITIONAL MOTIFS

Work same as First Motif through Rnd 3: 6 ch-4 sps.

Rnd 4 (Joining rnd)**:** With **right** side facing, join White with sc in any ch-4 sp; † ch 10, slip st in fourth ch from hook, ch 3, skip next 3 chs, slip st in next ch (**first Leaf made**), work Leaf 3 times †, ch 6, slip st in fourth ch from hook, ch 1, skip next ch, slip st in last ch (**joining Leaf made**), work Leaf, skip joining Leaf, slip st in base of next Leaf, (work Leaf, slip st in base of next Leaf) 3 times, slip st in next ch, ch 1, sc in next ch-4 sp, (ch 5, sc in next ch-4 sp) twice, repeat from † to † once, ch 4; holding Motifs with **wrong** sides together, sc in ch-3 sp at tip of joining Leaf on **previous Motif**, ch 1, skip next ch on **new Motif**, slip st in next ch, ch 1, skip next ch, slip st in last ch, work Leaf, skip joining Leaf, slip st in base of next Leaf, (work Leaf, slip st in base of next Leaf) 3 times, slip st in next ch, ch 1, (sc in next ch-4 sp, ch 5) twice; join with slip st to first sc, finish off.

Make as many Additional Motifs as needed for desired length.

BORDER
FIRST SIDE

Row 1: With **right** side facing, join White with slip st in ch-3 sp at tip of unworked joining Leaf on first Motif; ch 8 (**counts as first dtr plus ch 3**), dtr in same sp, † ch 1, (sc in next ch-3 sp at tip of next Leaf, ch 1) 4 times, (dc, ch 1) twice in next ch-5 sp, sc in same sp, ch 1, sc in next ch-5 sp, ch 1, (dc in same sp, ch 1) twice, (sc in next ch-3 sp at tip of next Leaf, ch 1) 4 times †, ★ (dtr, ch 3, dtr) in same sp as next joining, repeat from † to † once; repeat from ★ across to last joining Leaf, (dtr, ch 3, dtr) in ch-3 sp at tip of last joining Leaf, leave remaining Leaves unworked.

Row 2: Ch 1, turn; sc in first dtr, ch 1, skip next ch, sc in next ch, ch 1, skip next ch, ★ sc in next st, ch 1, (skip next ch, sc in next st, ch 1) across to next ch-3 sp, skip next ch, sc in next ch, ch 1, skip next ch; repeat from ★ across to last dtr, sc in last dtr; finish off.

SECOND SIDE
Work same as First Side.

BROWN-EYED SUSANS   Approximate Width: 1¼" (3.25 cm)

STITCH GUIDE

BEGINNING CLUSTER (uses same st)
Ch 2, ★ YO, insert hook in same st, YO and pull up a loop, YO and draw through 2 loops on hook; repeat from ★ once **more**, YO and draw through all 3 loops on hook.

CLUSTER (uses one st)
★ YO, insert hook in st indicated, YO and pull up a loop, YO and draw through 2 loops on hook; repeat from ★ 2 times **more**, YO and draw through all 4 loops on hook.

FLOWER

With Brown, ch 4; join with slip st to form a ring.

Rnd 1 (Right side): Ch 3 **(counts as first dc)**, 11 dc in ring; join with slip st to first dc, finish off: 12 dc.

Note: Loop a short piece of thread around any stitch to mark Rnd 1 as **right** side.

Rnd 2: With **right** side facing, join Yellow with slip st in any dc; work beginning Cluster, ch 2, (work Cluster in next dc, ch 2) around; join with slip st to top of beginning Cluster, finish off: 12 ch-2 sps.

Make as many Flowers as needed for desired length, allowing approximately ¼" (6 mm) between each Flower.

BORDER

Joining Rnd: With **right** side of each Flower facing, join Green with sc in any ch-2 sp of First Flower *(see Joining With Sc, page 94)*; (sc, ch 3, 2 sc) in same sp, † (2 sc, ch 3, 2 sc) in next 4 ch-2 sps, 3 sc in next ch-2 sp on same Flower **and** in any ch-2 sp on next Flower †; repeat from † to † across to last 11 ch-2 sps on last Flower, (2 sc, ch 3, 2 sc) in next 5 ch-2 sps changing to White in last sc made *(Fig. 4, page 95)*, (2 sc, ch 3, 2 sc) in next 5 ch-2 sps, 3 sc in next ch-2 sp on same Flower **and** in first unworked ch-2 sp on next Flower, ★ (2 sc, ch 3, 2 sc) in next 4 ch-3 sps, 3 sc in next ch-2 sp on same Flower **and** in first unworked ch-2 sp on next Flower; repeat from ★ across to last 5 ch-2 sps, (2 sc, ch 3, 2 sc) in last 5 ch-3 sps; join with slip st to first sc, finish off.

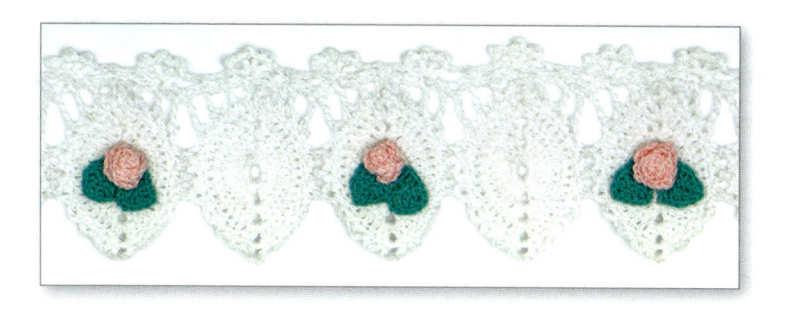

VICTORIAN ROSEBUDS   Approximate Width: 3" (7.5 cm)

ADDITIONAL SUPPLIES: Tapestry needle

STITCH GUIDE
TREBLE CROCHET
   (abbreviated tr)
YO twice, insert hook in sp indicated, YO and pull up a loop (4 loops on hook), (YO and draw through 2 loops on hook) 3 times.

DOUBLE TREBLE CROCHET
   (abbreviated dtr)
YO 3 times, insert hook in sp indicated, YO and pull up a loop (5 loops on hook), (YO and draw through 2 loops on hook) 4 times.

PICOT
Ch 3, sc in third ch from hook.

FIRST MOTIF
With White, ch 6; join with slip st to form a ring.

Rnd 1 (Right side): Ch 3 **(counts as first dc, now and throughout)**, 10 dc in ring, ch 2, 11 dc in ring, ch 1, sc in first dc to form last ch-2 sp: 22 dc and 2 ch-2 sps.

Note: Loop a short piece of thread around any stitch to mark Rnd 1 as **right** side.

Rnd 2: Ch 3, dc in last ch-2 sp made and in next 11 dc, (2 dc, ch 2, 2 dc) in next ch-2 sp, dc in next 11 dc, 2 dc in same sp as first dc, ch 1, sc in first dc to form last ch-2 sp: 30 dc and 2 ch-2 sps.

Rnd 3: Ch 3, dc in last ch-2 sp made and in next 15 dc, (2 dc, ch 2, 2 dc) in next ch-2 sp, dc in next 15 dc, 2 dc in same sp as first dc, hdc in first dc to form last ch-2 sp: 38 dc and 2 ch-2 sps.

87

Rnd 4: Ch 1, (sc, ch 5, sc) in last ch-2 sp made, † skip next dc, (sc, ch 3, sc) in next dc †; repeat from † to † 5 times **more**, place marker around last ch-3 made for joining placement, repeat from † to † 3 times, skip next dc, (sc, ch 5, sc) in next ch-2 sp, repeat from † to † 7 times, place marker around last ch-3 made for Border placement, repeat from † to † twice, skip last dc; join with slip st to first sc, finish off.

ADDITIONAL MOTIFS

Work same as First Motif through Rnd 3: 38 dc and 2 ch-2 sps.

Rnd 4 (Joining rnd)**:** Ch 1, (sc, ch 5, sc) in same sp, † skip next dc, (sc, ch 3, sc) in next dc †; repeat from † to † 5 times **more**, place marker around last ch-3 made for joining placement, repeat from † to † 3 times, skip next dc, (sc, ch 5, sc) in next ch-2 sp, repeat from † to † 3 times, skip next dc, sc in next dc, ch 1; with **wrong** sides of Motifs together, sc in marked ch-3 sp on **previous Motif**, ch 1, sc in same st on **new Motif**, ★ skip next dc, sc in next dc, ch 1, sc in next ch-3 sp on **previous Motif**, ch 1, sc in same st on **new Motif**; repeat from ★ once **more**, then repeat from † to † 3 times, skip last dc; join with slip st to first sc, finish off.

Make as many Additional Motifs as needed for desired length less 1$^7/_8$" (4.75 cm), working an odd number of Additional Motifs.

LAST MOTIF

Work same as First Motif through Rnd 3: 38 dc and 2 ch-2 sps.

Rnd 4 (Joining rnd)**:** Ch 1, (sc, ch 5, sc) in last ch-2 sp made, skip next dc, † (sc, ch 3, sc) in next dc, skip next dc †; repeat from † to † across to next ch-2 sp, (sc, ch 5, sc) in ch-2 sp, skip next dc, repeat from † to † 3 times, sc in next dc, ch 1; with **wrong** sides of Motifs together, sc in marked ch-3 sp on **previous Motif**, ch 1, sc in same st on **new Motif**, skip next dc, ★ sc in next dc, ch 1, sc in next ch-3 sp on **previous Motif**, ch 1, sc in same st on **new Motif**, skip next dc; repeat from ★ once **more**, then repeat from † to † 3 times; join with slip st to first sc, finish off.

BORDER

Row 1: With **right** side facing, join White with slip st in marked ch-3 sp on First Motif; ch 7 (**counts as first dtr plus ch 2**), tr in next ch-3 sp, ch 2, dc in next ch-3 sp, ch 2, sc in next ch-5 sp, ch 2, dc in next ch-3 sp, ch 2, tr in next ch-3 sp, ch 2, dtr in next ch-3 sp, ★ skip next joining, dtr in next ch-3 sp, ch 2, tr in next ch-3 sp, ch 2, dc in next ch-3 sp, ch 2, sc in next ch-5 sp, ch 2, dc in next ch-3 sp, ch 2, tr in next ch-3 sp, ch 2, dtr in next ch-3 sp; repeat from ★ across.

Row 2: Ch 1, turn; sc in first dtr, ch 2, (skip next ch-2 sp, sc in next st, ch 2) 5 times, ★ skip next dtr, sc in sp **before** next dtr *(Fig. 3, page 95)*, ch 2, (skip next ch-2 sp, sc in next st, ch 2) 5 times; repeat from ★ across to last dtr, sc in last dtr.

Row 3: Ch 1, turn; sc in first sc, ch 2, dc in next sc, (work Picot, dc in same st) 3 times, ch 2, ★ skip next sc, sc in next sc, ch 2, skip next sc, dc in next sc, (work Picot, dc in same st) 3 times, ch 2; repeat from ★ across to last sc, sc in last sc; finish off.

ROSE AND LEAVES

Make one Rose and 2 Leaves for every other Motif.

ROSE

Row 1 (Right side)**:** With Pink, ch 20, (sc, ch 3, sc) in second ch from hook, ★ skip next ch, (sc, ch 3, sc) in next ch; repeat from ★ across; finish off leaving a long end for sewing.

With **right** side facing and beginning in first sc, roll piece tightly to form Rose. Thread tapestry needle with thread end and stitch through base several times to secure.

LEAF

Row 1 (Right side)**:** With Green, ch 7, Dc in fourth ch from hook and in next ch, hdc in next ch, 3 sc in last ch; working in free loops of beginning ch *(Fig. 2, page 94)*, hdc in next ch, dc in next dc, (dc, ch 3, slip st) in same ch as first dc; finish off leaving a long end for sewing.

Using photo as a guide, page 87, sew Roses and Leaves to Motifs.

89

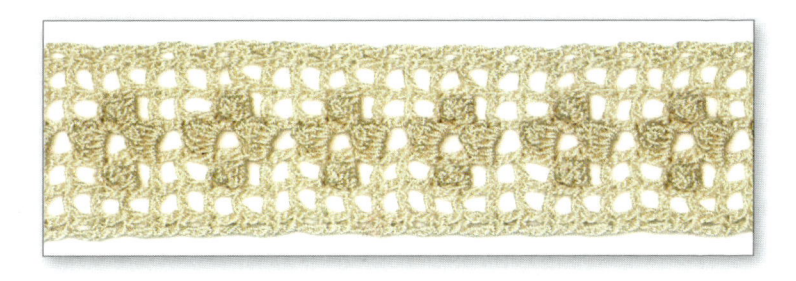

POPCORN BAND

Approximate Width: 1¾" (4.5 cm)

STITCH GUIDE

POPCORN (uses one sp)
5 Dc in sp indicated, drop loop from hook, insert hook from the **right** side in first dc of 5-dc group, hook dropped loop and draw through st, ch 1 to close. Push through to **right** side if needed.

INSTRUCTIONS

Row 1 (Right side)**:** Ch 20, dc in fourth ch from hook, ch 2, skip next 2 chs, ★ dc in next ch, ch 2, skip next 2 chs; repeat from ★ 3 times **more**, dc in last 2 chs: 5 ch-2 sps.

Row 2: Ch 3 **(counts as first dc, now and throughout)**, turn; dc in next dc, (ch 2, dc in next dc) twice, work Popcorn in next ch-2 sp, (dc in next dc, ch 2) twice, dc in next dc and in top of beginning ch: 4 ch-2 sps.

Row 3: Ch 3, turn; dc in next dc, ch 2, ★ dc in next dc, work Popcorn in next ch-2 sp, dc in next dc, ch 2; repeat from ★ once **more**, dc in last 2 dc: 3 ch-2 sps.

Row 4: Ch 3, turn; dc in next dc, (ch 2, dc in next dc) twice, work Popcorn in next ch-2 sp, (dc in next dc, ch 2) twice, dc in last 2 dc: 4 ch-2 sps.

Row 5: Ch 3, turn; (dc in next dc, ch 2) across to last 2 dc, dc in last 2 dc: 5 ch-2 sps.

Row 6: Ch 3, turn; dc in next dc, (ch 2, dc in next dc) twice, work Popcorn in next ch-2 sp, (dc in next dc, ch 2) twice, dc in last 2 dc: 4 ch-2 sps.

Repeat Rows 3-6 for desired length, ending by working Row 5; finish off.

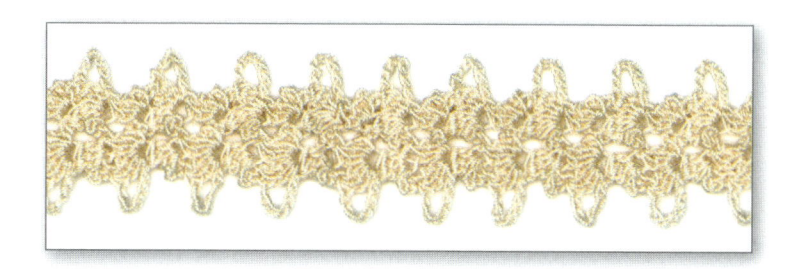

PICOT BAND

Approximate Width: 1¼" (3.25 cm)

STITCH GUIDE

CLUSTER (uses one st)
★ YO, insert hook in st indicated, YO and pull up a loop, YO and draw through 2 loops on hook; repeat from ★ 2 times **more**, YO and draw through all 4 loops on hook.

PICOT
Ch 4, sc in fourth ch from hook.

INSTRUCTIONS

Row 1 (Right side)**:** Ch 11, work (Cluster, Picot) twice in eighth ch from hook, skip next 2 chs, work Cluster in last ch: 3 Clusters.

Row 2: Ch 7, turn; work (Cluster, Picot) twice in first Cluster, skip next Picot, work Cluster in next Cluster, leave remaining Cluster unworked.

Repeat Row 2 for desired length; finish off.

RICKRACK LACE

Approximate Width: 1 1/8" (2.75 cm)

STITCH GUIDE
DECREASE
Pull up a loop in each of next 2 sc, YO and draw through all 3 loops on hook.

FOUNDATION
Row 1: Ch 11, dc in eighth ch from hook, ch 2, skip next 2 chs, dc in last ch: 2 ch-sps.

Row 2: Ch 5, turn; dc in next dc, ch 2, skip next 2 chs, dc in next ch.

Row 3: Ch 10, turn; dc in eighth ch from hook, ch 2, skip next 2 chs, dc in next dc, leave remaining sts unworked.

Repeat Rows 2 and 3 for desired length, ending by working Row 2; do **not** finish off.

EDGING
Rnd 1: Ch 1, turn; sc in first dc, 2 sc in next ch-2 sp, † 9 sc in next ch-sp, (2 sc in each of next 2 sps, 9 sc in next ch-sp) across to end sp, 2 sc in end sp †, sc in first free loop of beginning ch *(Fig. 2, page 94)*, tie a scrap piece of thread around sc just made, 2 sc in same sp, repeat from † to † once; join with slip st to first sc.

Rnd 2 (Right side)**:** Ch 1, turn; sc in same st, decrease, sc in next 4 sc, 3 sc in next sc, sc in next 4 sc, (decrease twice, sc in next 4 sc, 3 sc in next sc, sc in next 4 sc) across to within 2 sc of marked sc, decrease, 3 sc in marked sc, decrease, sc in next 4 sc, 3 sc in next sc, sc in next 4 sc, (decrease twice, sc in next 4 sc, 3 sc in next sc, sc in next 4 sc) across to last 3 sc, decrease, 3 sc in last sc; join with slip st to first sc, finish off.

GENERAL INSTRUCTIONS

ABBREVIATIONS

ch(s)	chain(s)
cm	centimeters
dc	double crochet(s)
dtr	double treble crochet(s)
hdc	half double crochet(s)
mm	millimeters
Rnd(s)	Round(s)
sc	single crochet(s)
sp(s)	space(s)
st(s)	stitch(es)
tr	treble crochet(s)
YO	yarn over

SYMBOLS & TERMS

★ — work instructions following ★ as many **more** times as indicated in addition to the first time.

† to † — work all instructions from first † to second † **as many** times as specified.

( ) or [ ] — work enclosed instructions **as many** times as specified by the number immediately following **or** work all enclosed instructions in the stitch or space indicated **or** contains explanatory remarks.

colon (:) — the number(s) given after a colon at the end of a row or round denote(s) the number of stitches or spaces you should have on that row or round.

CROCHET TERMINOLOGY

UNITED STATES		INTERNATIONAL
slip stitch (slip st)	=	single crochet (sc)
single crochet (sc)	=	double crochet (dc)
half double crochet (hdc)	=	half treble crochet (htr)
double crochet (dc)	=	treble crochet (tr)
treble crochet (tr)	=	double treble crochet (dtr)
double treble crochet (dtr)	=	triple treble crochet (ttr)
triple treble crochet (tr tr)	=	quadruple treble crochet (qtr)
skip	=	miss

STEEL CROCHET HOOKS

U.S.	00	0	1	2	3	4	5	6	7	8	9	10	11	12	13	14
Metric - mm	3.5	3.25	2.75	2.25	2.1	2	1.9	1.8	1.65	1.5	1.4	1.3	1.1	1	.85	.75

GAUGE

The edging instructions are written for bedspread weight cotton thread (size 10). Gauge is not of great importance; your edgings may be a little larger or smaller without changing the overall effect.

MULTIPLES

Some of the patterns are worked for a multiple of rows to enable the Edging on the end of rows to work. An example is Pearl Drops on page 39, which is worked for a multiple of 3 + 1 row. The pattern would require 4, 7, 10, 13 rows, or any number divisible by 3 plus an additional row.

JOINING WITH SC

When instructed to join with sc, begin with a slip knot on hook. Insert hook in stitch or space indicated, YO and pull up a loop, YO and draw through both loops on hook.

BACK RIDGE

Work only in loops indicated by arrows *(Fig. 1)*.

Fig. 1

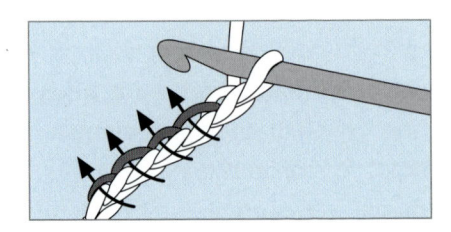

FREE LOOPS OF A CHAIN

When instructed to work in free loops of a chain, work in loop indicated by arrow *(Fig. 2)*.

Fig. 2

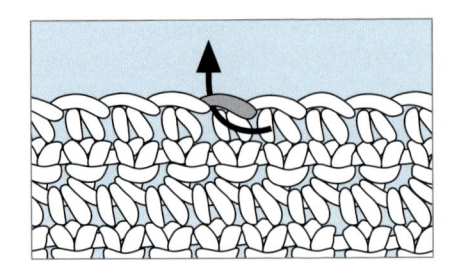

WORKING IN SPACE BEFORE A STITCH

When instructed to work in a space **before** a stitch or in a space **between** stitches, insert hook in space indicated by arrow *(Fig. 3)*.

Fig. 3

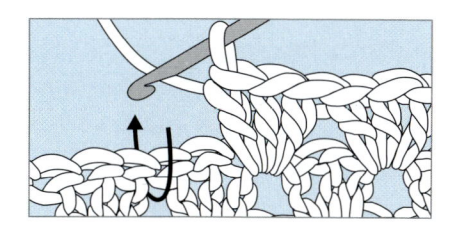

CHANGING COLORS

Work the last stitch to within one step of completion, hook new thread *(Fig. 4)* and draw through all loops on hook.

Fig. 4

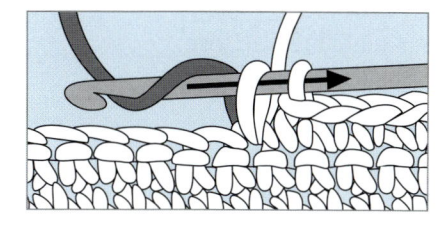

WASHING AND BLOCKING

For a more professional look, edgings should be washed and blocked. Using a mild detergent and warm water and being careful not to rub, twist, or wring, gently squeeze suds through the piece. Rinse several times in cool, clear water. Roll piece in a clean terry towel and gently press out the excess moisture. Lay piece on a flat surface and shape to proper size; where needed, pin in place using rust-proof pins. Allow to dry **completely**.

THREAD INFORMATION

The Edgings in this book were made using Aunt Lydia's® Crochet Thread™ Classic 10™, a Bedspread Weight Cotton Thread. Any brand of bedspread weight cotton thead (size 10) may be used.

For your convenience, listed below are the specific colors used to create our photography models. Because yarn/thread manufacturers make frequent changes in their product lines, you may sometimes find it necessary to use a substitute thread/color or to search for the discontinued product at alternate suppliers (locally or online).

#1 White
#12 Black
#131 Fudge Brown
#226 Natural
#401 Orchid Pink
#419 Ecru
#422 Golden Yellow
#423 Maize

#450 Aqua
#458 Purple
#480 Delft
#492 Burgundy
#493 French Rose
#494 Victory Red
#495 Wood Violet
#661 Frosty Green